I
Turn to
Prayer

brown bridges press

First Edition

1. Body Mind Spirit 2. Spiritual Life. 3. Metaphysics 4. New Thought 5. Self Help
6. Devotions. 7. Meditations. 8. Christian Life

"The prayer of faith is an unconditional belief in both the ability and the desire of Spirit to hear and answer. The prayer of faith heals the sick through the law which says that whatever images of thought are held in the subjective side of mind will tend to appear in the body, or in the body of affairs."

Ernest Holmes

Acknowledgements

How fitting it is that at that moment when I thought this book might not happen I turned to the power of prayer. I asked Marsha Woodard; Sandra Francis; Kym King; Susan Pahnke; Chris Terry; Brynde Lambert; Erin Fry; Andriette Earl and Diane Consolino to hold the completion of this book in prayer. Their prayerful consciousness kept me moving forward.

In addition to those listed above I am especially grateful for Anita Pickinpaugh. She refused to be distracted by my doubts. She knew when I was busy with appointments, meetings, travel and other commitments that no thing and no one would get in the way of this book being birthed. I am so grateful for her belief, for her prayers and for her encouraging emails during the final weeks.

And the cover photo? It represents the amazing talent of Jim Duncan. For more than 10 years he brought his heart, as well as his talent, to every photo shoot and captured not only my image but also my essence. I am grateful. Now he is retired as a photographer but he will never retire from bringing his love of God into everything he does.

Contents

Ways to Use This Book

The prayers in this book are not organized by subject. I found that often a prayer that seemed to be about money was equally a prayer about peace. Or a prayer about joy was just as much a prayer for balance or growth.

So my prayer is that you will find yourself intuitively guided to the exact page that will serve you best each time you pick up this book.

A few suggestions to consider:

1. Scan the Table of Contents for a title that resonates with you or a title that seems related to whatever you want prayer for.

2. Or you might open the book to a random page and read that prayer or a few prayers in that section of the book.

3. You could use the book to guide your daily spiritual practice by reading 1-3 prayers each day for a week or a month. Since all the prayers are inspired by universal spiritual principles you might be surprised at which prayers "speak" to you and bring you insight or inspiration.

4. Another option would be sharing the book with a friend or prayer partner. Set a specific time each week to reflect together and discuss one or more prayers that relate to whatever you are experiencing that week.

5. And of course, you can use these prayers not only for your own spiritual grounding, but also for sharing with family members and friends as they are going through the ups and downs of life.

Introduction

Prayer changes *our* consciousness, not God's.

Think about it: If you were omnipotent, omnipresent and omniscient what would there be to worry about? You would know everything that has ever happened, everything that could ever happen and of course, everything that is happening right now. And you would see how it was all working together for Good and what needed to be adjusted so that the best and highest expression of Life would unfold.

God's consciousness is one of love and wisdom and order. There is no worry or fear or panic or confusion in God.

On the other hand, think about our consciousness. We feed ourselves a constant diet of fear, limitation and separation. We get all caught up in the human experience and forget our true, essential nature is that of spiritual beings.

Prayer reminds us of what is possible and who we truly are.

So it's us, not God, who is changed by prayer.

"Be careful for nothing; but in everything (by prayer and supplication with thanksgiving) let your requests be made known unto God." (Philippians 4:6)

Many of the prayers in this book follow a five-step prayer process described in the teachings of Ernest Holmes and Science of Mind.

1. Recognition: I recognize there is one God and that God is the perfect example of all Good.

2. Unification: I cannot be separated from God; my life is unified with God's life.

3. Realization: God's presence is reflected in my life in physical, emotional, mental and spiritual outcomes. What I declare and believe manifests in my experience of life.

4. Thanksgiving: I am grateful for spiritual knowledge and for my unfolding life.

5. Release: I know this is all done based on Universal spiritual principals and I am willing to allow God to work in my life.

This, or a similar sequence, can be found in prayers from a variety of faiths. I use this process simply because it provides a structure that encourages me to first acknowledge God, then recognize my relationship to the Divine before clarifying that which I want to experience in my life. This is followed by an expression of my gratitude and a recommitment to act in faith.

But prayers can take many forms. When I remember that the purpose of prayer is to create a shift in consciousness (from believing in human limitations to recognizing Divine incarnation in the physical world) then I can easily release my attachment to any single format or structure.

So a section of this book includes prayers written as poems. Poetry and journaling are both a big part of my prayer practice, for some prayers defy structure and simply insist on being expressed in creative ways.

And in a 21st century approach, I have also included a few prayers written in 140-characters or less. These are designed to encourage sharing prayer via Twitter, in text messages or in other electronic forms.

If you have ever needed a prayer but didn't know where to turn, this book is for you. If you have felt like your own prayers aren't working and you need the support of an experienced prayer partner, you will find this book helpful. And if you just enjoy affirmative prayer as part of your spiritual practice, you will find inspiration in these pages.

Overall, it is my prayer that you are renewed daily by the power of prayer. May you find prayers that resonate with you within this collection. May you be inspired to write and speak your own prayers. And may you choose to use prayer as a personal, private pathway to a deeper relationship with your own Divine nature.

Because you are reading this book I know my prayer has already been answered. And because we are all connected, your prayer is now my prayer too.

Tracy Brown

April 2014

I
Turn to
Prayer

Affirmative Prayer

"You pray in your distress and in your need; would that you might pray also in the fullness of your joy and in your days of abundance."

—Kahlil Gibran

Faith

God is always present, all powerful, all knowing. God is the constant inhale and exhale. God is all there is.

I am one with this constancy that can never fail. I am one with this constancy that is always present and contains all the wisdom of the ages.

So I affirm my intention to go through today in complete faith that all my needs ARE met. I know this intention simply reflects the simple Truth that God is always present and that God never fails.

I know that God is NOT a 9-1-1 energy simply swooping in to save me from chaos and ruin. No! God is an eternal presence that operates in me, as me and through me. God is experiencing this situation as me and knowing exactly what to do and when to do it.

So my story about stress and my false belief in fear are released in this moment. I am telling a new story about Divine Order and focusing my belief in faith. I have the faith of God because God is expressing in me as eternal Wisdom and there is NOTHING that is ever happening that is outside of that or smarter than that or more powerful that that!

I relax now in gratitude that the answer to my question is already present. I am grateful for knowing I can never have a problem that is too big or too scary for God to handle. I am grateful for knowing that I am standing in whatever gap exists knowing the Truth of me and the Truth of God is the same Truth.

So, with a deep breath, I just: LET. THIS. GO.

Yes! Complete!

Debt Free

There's only one life. That life is God's life. That life is Perfect.

That life is my life now.

There is no debt in God and so my natural state is one that is free of debt. I am on a life journey toward my best and highest good and I know my best and highest good includes responsible stewardship of money in a way that results in financial security.

I pay off my credit card debt quickly and easily. I manage my finances responsibly and my financial assets grow steadily.

I am grateful this truth is unfolding in, as and through my life. And I release anything that is out of alignment with a debt-free life.

Divine Activity is always expressing and always saying Yes. So I know this is already done in Divine Mind. I accept it. I allow it to be.

As it is spoken; so it is done.

Choosing My Path

There is One Power, One Presence, One Perfect Expression of Life. It has no limits and cannot be contained by time or space, by shape or form. It is creative and always ready to be Love, Peace and Joy.

I am this Power expressing uniquely as me. I am an individualization of God. And I know and accept that each and every person is expressing this same power in ways unique and perfect for them.

I speak my word knowing that I am choosing which gates to go through and which opportunities to experience. There is no duplicate of me in the world and I have the freedom to choose my path!

I also know each person I come into contact with is inventing his or her own experience of Life. I know this is by Divine design and I celebrate it! I am humbled by the ways diversity within humanity reminds me of the unlimited creativity of God. I am so happy to know that each person I interact with expands my experience of the Divine.

So there is no need for me to compete with others because each person is simply God expressing in a unique way. There is no rank ordering of my chosen path compared to anyone else's journey through life because my journey is meant to be MY journey. I have no need to judge, direct or set the travel plan for any one else's life.

My intention is to sail out on my personal voyage of discovery, unleashing the unique and valuable ways God is able to express through me. And I choose to take responsibility for making decisions and taking actions that bring forth great love, perfect peace and deep joy in me and in the world.

So I release all fear that I can do it wrong. I get to direct my life and I can choose what is best for me. And I let go of any judgment of people whose paths are different from my own. I am willing to offer the gift of acceptance to the journeys that others choose for themselves. I know that my path is Divinely blessed and that all paths lead to God.

I am grateful there is a Power for Good in the Universe ... and I can use It. Spiritual Law is always conspiring for my Good. I am free to use the Creative Process to live a life I love. I am equally grateful for the opportunity to be an expression of love, peace and joy with every one I meet recognizing as they choose their path they are showing me the unlimited nature of God expressing uniquely in, as and through them.

I release these words, and this intention, into the flow of Divine activity and I know it is already in motion and being fulfilled.

And So It Is!

Wisdom and Divine Order

I breathe in and remember all I need is supplied. My inhale takes in exactly what is required for my body to function. My exhale releases all my body cannot use and offers it to different forms of life. This cycle of in and out, receive and give, was not created by me. I don't make it happen or will it to be so. This cycle is a powerful reminder of the wisdom and Divine Order of God.

I am completely connected to this Wisdom and this Divine Order. In fact, what I know for sure is that there is no way to break the connection between the Wisdom of God and me.

So it is into the consciousness of that Perfect Connection that I speak these words.

I know that I am a physical expression of Divine Wisdom and everything that is happening in my life today is being executed in Divine Order. How can it be any other way? I am full of God. I am the delight of God. I am the walking, talking, praying expression of God's wisdom in all I do. Today is no exception to that.

I claim that anything and everything that looks like a problem in my life is matched by a perfect solution or outcome. This must be so because all of life is about God expressing as good or for good.

I claim that anything and everything that brings forth fear in my mind is matched by perfect faith and a peace that is beyond human understanding. This must be so because all of life is about God expressing as love. A life lived within love is completely lived in peace.

I claim that anything and everything that shows up as lack or limitation in my heart is matched by abundance and prosperity. This must be so because all of life is about God expressing as growth and expansion. There is no standing still and there is no going backward in God's life.

I claim this all, knowing that the Universe does not need my approval nor my direction to do what it does. And what it always does is respond to the deepest desires and to the best and highest good for my life.

So I am grateful for the never ending YES provided by the Universe. Yes to me. Yes to Me. Yes to all of Life.

I release ... I let go ... And So It Is!

Healing Family Conflict

I know the Truth: All there is is God. One Power. One Intelligence. One Love.

I am that One Power, One Intelligence and One Love expressing in physical form. This same Power, Intelligence and Love is expressing in, as and through every member of my family.

I have an internal GPS that guides, guards and directs me as I resolve all misunderstandings with my family. I am blessed to be a healing presence. I reveal the Truth within myself and I provide grounding and support for my family members. I am a light in the darkness because I am shining God's Light. I am the quiet, deep peace in the storm of confusion because I am sharing God's Wisdom. I am a warm hug in the chill of fear because I am demonstrating God's Love.

I stand in the knowing that everything that is unfolding here is simply the best and highest good for each family member, and for me. I understand that the Truth of Spirit is operating always - and in all ways - through this situation. My intuition is simply the whisper of God guiding me to access the Intelligence that is within me. My strength is not my own; it is the Power of God coursing through every cell in my body. And my love for my family and for myself is simply the Love of God expressing with every pulse of every heartbeat.

So I release any connection to life being unfair or of being disrespected or any number of ways my human brain wants to tell me I should fight, disagree or see that I am being treated unfairly. What I know is that there is no fight or conflict or unfairness in God. In God there is only Love.

I choose to be love, to give love to my family members and to create a loving environment for myself.

I am so grateful for this Truth and Power. I am so grateful that Infinite Intelligence is always present. I am so grateful that I have made a commitment to be a beneficial presence bringing the deepest Love everywhere I go. I know this is sufficient. I know this is Good.

So I release this knowing into the flow of Divine Activity. I let it go. I let it be.

As it is spoken; so it is done.

Preparing for Baby's Birth

There is no spot where God is not. God is in every thought and every thing. God is in every space and every place. God is around and within every person. God is the presence of love, peace, wellness and joy.

And I know that this same presence of love, peace, wellness and joy exists in every cell of my body because I am simply the human expression of God. All that God is exists within me.

So, knowing that God is in every place, I claim God's presence in the delivery room as I welcome this child into the world. The obstetrician, the nurses, the aides, the assistants, the technicians, the clerks, the volunteers - in fact every person who has any connection to this delivery - is guided by the Wisdom and Love of Spirit.

I am fully grounded in the Spiritual Truth so I simply affirm that I am the perfect parent to serve as the human representative of Spirit's love for this child. I will not be distracted by any disturbances in my life because they are all temporary issues and concerns. I know the Spiritual Truth of Divine Love, Divine Wisdom, Divine Abundance and Divine Wellness prevail in this situation and always. It is inevitable and undeniable.

So I focus now on love and peace ... on wellness and joy. That is what is happening in this moment. Love expressed as a new life. This new life is welcomed into a family where peace creates a safe and nurturing environment. This nurturing environment promotes wellness in this child and in every family member. And all live in joy.

I am grateful to know there are no accidents or coincidences. This baby is born to express its health in the way that is perfect for him. I am grateful to be a part of this process where life transforms from a Divine Idea into a human baby.

And so I release my deepest desires for a healthy delivery with no complications to Universal Law. I let go and let God.

And So It Is.

Financial Stability

There is only one Source, one Spirit, one power. I call this Source God knowing there is no word big enough to contain all that It is. I know God is effortless abundance. I know God is Divine order. Nothing can occur that God cannot handle because all that is and all that happens occurs within the one Source, one Spirit and one power called God.

And because God expresses through me, I experience this effortless abundance and Divine order in my life every day.

The Truth of my experience is abundance and order. I receive enough money to pay all bills, save for emergencies and prepare financially for the expenses of my retirement years. I manage my finances easily and experience financial stability in all parts of my life. It is fun and easy to notice the abundance of the Universe flow to me and to use the resources provided to create financial stability in my life. I create and use money management techniques, systems and resources that insure I am prepared to handle any need or desire I might have.

Financial stability allows me to not only take care of my needs, but also to tithe and to generously give to others.

I am overflowing with gratitude for this Truth. Thank you Spirit for demonstrating abundance and Divine order in my life.

My word is powerful and true. And so that which I have spoken is already done . . . alive . . . and working . . . in my world now.

And So It Is.

Committed Relationship

Peace is the silence felt during meditation. Peace is that inner feeling of calm. Peace is the still water of a lake at morning sunrise. Peace is sitting on a bench in a beautiful, lush park on a warm spring day. Peace is simply another name for God expressing. God is the Perfect example of Peace.

And I have been made in the spiritual image and likeness of God so peace is within me, peace expresses as me and peace is shared through me. I can never be separated from Peace.

I know the Universe is always conspiring for my best and highest Good. And my good includes a committed relationship with the perfect person for me. I know the Universe is already actively working on delivering this – or something better – into my life.

I affirm that I have the power to define my life and the Universe simply says YES to that which I claim or demand. My desire is to experience this special relationship with my perfect mate knowing that in God ALL things are possible and I receive as I believe.

And so, I release any old story that expresses itself as worry or doubt, especially worry or doubt about relationships. I replace old doubt with the belief and the knowing that my request is already accepted and blessed by the Divine.

I am ready for this relationship and ready to allow myself to be the person I need to be to attract and experience this perfect relationship.

I am so grateful for this Good unfolding in my life.

And because I know the Law of Cause and Effect is ALWAYS working I set this cause in motion by delivering it into Universal Law with clarity and joyful expectation.

And So It Is!

Balancing Class, Work and Family

God. Spirit. Allah. Buddha. By any name It is the same. It is that life energy that knows no boundaries and provides the source for all of creation. What I know for sure is that all creation is from this Source and all creation from this Source is good. There is room and time for all that Spirit creates and comes alive in. All things and all choices grounded in Spirit are sufficiently provided for through right action, right energy, right choice, right time.

And I know I am totally one with this Divine source. All my choices and all my tasks are guided by my oneness with Divine energy and unlimited Source.

Every day I make the right choices that support my ability to complete all homework on time and still enjoy the other areas of my life. I easily prioritize and I enjoy every aspect of my class. I am enriched by the reading and inspired by the more reflective parts of each week's lesson. I prepare for each class while maintaining my responsibilities at work, continuing my involvement in community projects and finding time to enjoy family and friends. I intuitively know how to prioritize so I can experience those things which support my best and highest good.

It is clear to me when I should say "no" or "not now" so I am able to fulfill all commitments with joy and with excellence. It is easy to complete every assignment and every task I agree to complete with excellence and ease. Right action guides my every choice and each day is busy and balanced.

How sweet it is to relax and be grateful for the ability to walk through this class, and this life, guided by Spirit's voice. I am so thankful to know God works in me and through me as I go through each day.

And because these words are true and powerful and impossible to deny . . . I release them into the Universe and into my life. Letting the Law work, I affirm this Truth

And So It Is

Demonstrating Integrity

Spirit is the life energy of the universe. Spirit is in and of every thing that exists. Spirit is always in alignment with itself and all actions sourced in Spirit can only be good.

My source and my energy are one and same with Spirit.

Everything I do and say is in alignment with Spirit. It is easy for me to choose my actions and my priorities. It is equally easy for me to choose my boundaries. That which I promise to do I do, so I can meet my own expectations and the expectations of those who depend upon me.

With a quiet smile I recognize the deep gratitude I feel for being able to choose my actions and my priorities. I am so happy to be aligned with Spirit every moment of every day.

And knowing this is true today, tomorrow and always, I release it into right action. Now.

Amen.

Unlimited Abundance

Spirit is all there is. The Creator of all is all there is. All that exists is from Spirit and of Spirit; there are no limits upon what Spirit can be, can create or can provide. Spirit is limitless and generous. All created by Spirit have unlimited access to the good provided by and created by Spirit.

I am eligible for all the good provided by and created by Spirit because I am a part of that unlimited good. I can tap into my own good and be directly in the flow of limitless abundance.

I am a great example of the abundance and ever expanding good of Spirit. All my physical and emotional needs are provided for. I have the money and time I need to generously support people and programs I care about. I am always in the flow of good and receive an ever expanding portion of good. I am able to rely on an ever expanding reserve to provide all I need for as long as I live. This is true because there is no lack and there is no limitation in Spirit, or in me.

How exciting it is to know this Truth and to demonstrate it in small and big ways every day. I am grateful.

And there is nothing left for me to do but accept this truth and release it into the Law where it is already done. It is already good.

It is done.

Honoring the Ancestors

What I know about Spirit is that It is unlimited. Unlimited in wisdom. Unlimited in creativity. Unlimited in joy. Unlimited in love. Spirit intentionally created people in what seems like an infinite variation of shades, shapes and sensibilities.

I am made of the same stuff that Spirit is made of. I am a full and perfect creation designed to represent Spirit as only I can. I am different and unique from every other human expression of Spirit. I am one whole, perfect and complete expression of Spirit.

I am black and female because Spirit created me as me: a talented, generous, smart and peaceful African American woman. I am a physical descendant of a long line of spiritually guided warriors who survived all kinds of human atrocities because they knew (and passed down to me) the unbreakable inner strength of Spirit. I am a link in a long chain of people who listened to the voice of Spirit and ignored the words of human power.

I know I am here to fulfill a Divine purpose that only I can fill. I am able to make a positive difference in this world. I am a beneficial presence in the world. I am Spirit walking around gifting people with a smile, a listening ear and a little reminder that we all have a choice.

There is no coincidence that I do the work I do; my earliest memories are filled with experiences where I was judged based on stereotypes about my race, my health, my gender and my place in the world. But I am not so much a survivor as a cartographer mapping a better road through the jungles of life.

Every day I remember I don't have to know anything about anyone I come into contact with; I only need to know, and trust, the guidance of Spirit. I am the perfect representation of the wisdom, creativity, joy and love of Spirit, in this place at this time to show up and show out! I am my history and my future, and it's all good.

Because I know this, I can relax and let the Law do all the work. So I inhale the always present breath of Spirit and release this Truth with my next exhale.

As it is spoken; so it is done.

Intimate, Loving Relationship

I believe in one God, one Creator, one Divine Being of Light. This Divine Being is the source of all good and all of life.

My life is God's life. God is the source and the soul and the substance of every aspect of my life.

Therefore, any intention I set is already held in the spirit, soul and body of God. I now set the intention to experience intimacy in a relationship where I and my partner experience expansive love, joy, peace and prosperity together. I know I am right now becoming a powerful magnet for this person who is my perfect vibrational match. I release any belief in limitations, any attachment to contrast as a necessary experience and any fear that intimacy must result in pain. I turn instead to the promise of love, the connection of trust, the power of faith and the clarity of Divine Order. I accept that the moment I knew what to pray for I set a new cause into motion.

I am so grateful that Spirit is never distracted by anything that is out of alignment with my best and highest Good.

So I release these words into Divine Activity knowing it is already done.

And So It Is.

Facing a Challenge

The perfect example of wisdom, strength, peace and joy is God.

There is no question that my true nature is one of wisdom and strength balanced perfectly by peace and joy.

So I know that I am able to face any challenge presented knowing there is no challenge too big for God ... and that truly, in the circle of God no challenge exists because that would imply a good and a bad or an easy and a hard. The truth is that within the circle of God there is always and only balance and freedom.

I know the path to balance and freedom means letting go of the weeds and false beliefs that have grown around the Truth of me as protection, as direction and as comfort. I release my connection to that which no longer serves me. I allow it to fall away so I can experience that which I truly desire. I welcome the experience of change and loss for it is not a threat to my identity as much as it is allowing the emergence of my True Identity.

So I gratefully accept this process as a gift to me so I can see my own talents and my own Truth more clearly. I celebrate my deep and abiding faith and know I cannot be moved from knowing the Power and Presence of God in all of Life including this situation!

I acknowledge that everything that is in alignment with my best and highest good is now unfolding and I release these words into that Truth.

Amen. And So It Is!

When a Relationship Ends

The energy of God is Love. God sees Love in all people and God knows there is Love in every situation. God is always Love expressing and is always creating from Love. God is the example of Perfect Love.

I am one with God and so every cell in my body includes the blueprint for Love. The Love of God expresses throughout my life and can never be removed.

I set a clear intention right now to be love, to give love and to share love. I know that every relationship I engage in is not guaranteed to last my entire life. But I choose to be an expression of love in every relationship I am involved in.

When relationships end, or change from one form into another, I bless the time we have spent together and focus on the blessings and gifts I have received from knowing that person.

I stand here refusing to be fooled into believing that hurt, pain and tears last forever. I believe in a God-centered Universe where hurt is replaced by help. Pain is removed through prayer. And tears soon fade away because trust and faith prevail.

I turn away from the fog of fear and hurt and turn toward the bright sunlight of what I know to be true: that Spirit has never abandoned me, and will never abandon me. I know that Spirit is the Source of everything I need. And I know that Spirit provides every thing I need to care for myself, love myself and prepare myself for a relationship that is perfect for me.

I go into every relationship whole, perfect and complete. I leave each relationship whole, perfect and complete. I am always growing and everything is always unfolding for my good.

I breathe deeply and relax into the knowing that Spirit is well pleased with the life It is experiencing through me. Spirit never takes a day off. Spirit never turns Its back. Spirit never puts

www.ITurnToPrayer.com

25

anyone on hold. Spirit never says no. I am grateful for knowing I am guided, guarded and protected by Spirit at all times.

So I just relax into the guarantee that all is well. I let it go and let it be.

And So It Is.

Grounded in Peace

One thing I know for sure is the Creator of all is a loving Spirit. I know Spirit is both the storm and the calm after the storm. I know Spirit is the unlimited, universal Source for all that happens and I know that all that happens is either good - or leading to good. Spirit orchestrates and navigates all change grounded in Peace, for change is a natural part of the always expanding nature of Life.

I am one with Spirit on this journey called human life. So in times of change I too am grounded in Peace.

I am at peace. I am protected by Spirit through every trial I face. I invite each challenge and look for the lessons that deepen my spiritual growth.

I embrace each disappointment as an opportunity to learn or grow. My serenity and peace is firmly rooted in the depth of my soul and grounds me when people and events threaten my comfort.

This is the undeniable truth for which I am grateful.

And knowing peace has no opposite in God, I yield to the guidance and creative Power of Spirit.

As it is spoken; so it is done.

One

One love, one Source, one Power, one Presence. And with each breath, I breathe in this love, this source this power and this presence.

This is me. This love permeates every cell of my body. This source provides all I need and all I am. This power is my essence, my very being. This presence is my walk and my talk in this experience of life.

I am love. I am source. I am power. I am presence. And from this very moment I breathe this truth for myself and for all of life.

I breathe this truth for my family, friends and neighbors. I breathe this truth for my coworkers. I breathe this truth for leaders, for politicians and for the entire world.

I know there is one love, one sources, one power and one presence and it expresses through me. It expresses as me. It expresses in me. And it connects me with love to every other form of life.

I am grateful to know this is true.

I claim it; I exclaim it. I repeat it; I release it.

And So It Is

Peace First

I stand firmly in Peace for I know the peace of God is in every breath. I know the peace of God is in every creative idea. I know the peace of God is in every situation. I know the Universe is always conspiring for good.

I have been born from the Mind of God and so my good is the wish and the action of the Universe.

So this condition, this problem, this experience that I am in the middle of is happening but it does not define me. Clearly I am being shaped and molded for a purpose I cannot see. Clearly I am being grown in faith. And surely I am guided through all of this by Spirit Itself.

No condition, no experience, no loss and no gain can define the essential nature of this Divine One I am expressing. The one Divine life is always expressing in, as and through every human experience.

So I release all attachments to fear. I release all attachment to shame. I release all attachment to hopelessness. I release all attachment to life as it has been in the past. And I replace all of that with peace.

I demand the way be shown to walk through this in peace. I demand that I be provided everything I need to experience the best and highest outcome. I know I am Divinely guarded, guided and directed ... and no harm can come to me or through me.

I choose to be a dynamic example of faith in action. I am a consistent vessel of love and leadership. God is expressing in me, as me and through me in every moment. And so the intentions I have set must be fulfilled by the Universe.

This is my prayer. This is my knowing. This is my Truth and I shall not be moved from this place of faith. This place of faith is by its very nature a place of peace. And standing in peace I know there is nothing and no one but God showing up right now ... and always.

So I am grateful for whatever is unfolding here. I don't know what is happening for it is not of my design. But I know that everything that is happening must lead to a good so powerful it reveals the wisdom and love of Spirit in a deep and moving way.

I take these words and this intention into the deepest corner of my heart and release it from my control into the heartbeat of Life Itself: Divine Activity breathing peace, wholeness, wellness and abundance into me ... and into all of Creation.

Yes! This is Done!

Healing Eyesight

There is only one God. That God only knows health.

There is only one God. That God sees everything clearly.

Because I am an expression of this God living in human form, I now releases all past barriers to perfect health.

In this moment, I begin to reconnect my eyesight and my overall health to the perfect health I am entitled to as an incarnation of God.

I see myself happy and calm with restored sight. I am confident and see the world clearly.

I love what I see when I look in the mirror and appreciate what I see as I observe the outer world.

I choose to be a patient patient. I follow each step of treatment with commitment and with grace as I release all known (and unknown) fears that might interrupt the healing process.

I experience maximum healing not only of my eyes but also of my heart and soul. There is nothing to worry about and nothing to fear.

With deep, deep gratitude I am thankful for knowing my Word is the most powerful catalyst for change in my life and in the world.

I can totally relax now, knowing the Law hears this word and has already begun to shift the molecules in my body and in the minds and hands of my doctors to affirm the Truth of full and perfect healing for me.

This is done . . . with ease and grace. And So It Is.

Healing Money Worries

The unlimited energy that supplies all good and breathes life into all of creation is called by many names. It is known as Jehovah, as Allah, as Buddha, as Krishna, as Love, as Beauty, as Wholeness, as Peace. I call it Spirit; I call it God; and I know that any name I use is not big enough to capture It's unlimited and perfect nature.

There is no lack in God so this same condition of unlimited supply is my birthright for I am made of God stuff and the perfect balance of all Good is a part of my DNA.

So I set this intention knowing it must be made manifest.

I am at peace with money. When bills arrive I pay them in full. The money I need is already created and in circulation on its way to me. I have the money required to pay all bills, to save for retirement, to do fun things and to help others.

One of the benefits of having financial resources is philanthropy. I am full of peace about money; it is just a tool and resource to help me live a life that is full and fabulous! Money is just one tool in my toolkit for creating a better world for myself and for others.

I am not afraid of money. I am not afraid of wealth. I release all limiting beliefs that might contradict the truth that my supply of money is as unlimited as my Source.

I am grateful for this awareness that my relationship with money is healthy and productive. I am grateful for understanding there is no lack in God so there can be no lack in me.

So I release this intention into Perfect expression.

And So It Is.

Aging Gracefully

Spirit is the energy present in all things and in all people. Spirit created all there is. There is nothing designed by Spirit that has no purpose; all creatures and all forms have meaning and function.

I am one with Spirit and know my life and my body both have perfect meaning and perfect function.

My body is perfect and always changing. When I was a child I had a child's body. When I was a teen I had a teen's body. When I became a woman I had a woman's body. At every state of my life my body perfectly transforms to support my needs.

I am grateful for this body. I love the way my body supports me through the miracle of aging.

And I release this into the Law of the Universe.

As it is spoken, so it is done.

Comfort with Diversity

God is all there is. God is in everything experiencing Life as each person, each animal, each plant, each religion, each philosophy, and each idea. There is no idea in the Universe that did not originate in the Mind of God. And so, every idea – and every incarnation of those ideas, is truly and totally of God.

I am simply one perfect incarnation of the Mind of God. I am an example of the limitless capability of God showing up in the world as a unique expression.

And I know that every other person I meet, and every idea I am exposed to, is also a perfect incarnation of the Mind of God.

I am comfortable and at ease with the reality that people who make different decisions, have different beliefs, and live different experiences because I know each of these people are living their own God-experience the way they have been designed to live it.

I am aware that all people, animals, plants, philosophies, religions, beliefs and experiences may be different from my own experience or choice and they are still, with no exceptions, an experience of God.

I am thankful to be able to relax and stop trying to be in charge of all that is going on in the world because I know it is all working exactly as it should be in the Mind of God.

So, taking a deep breath of release, I allow the Law to do what it does so well.

Amen

Claiming My Health

Now. In this moment. I am reminded that all that is, is God, is Spirit, is Love. God is love and love is all there is. There is no dis-ease in God.

I am one with this God; one with this Love. I am this Spirit expressing in human form and so, there can be no disease within me.

I am not my father, my brother, my mother, my sister, my uncles, my aunts. I am an individual expression of the One that only knows health. Every cell of my body rejects disease and any cell that is experiencing distortion in any way is now healed and working perfectly. All systems and all organs in my body work together effortlessly to support a busy, vibrant, healthy and fulfilling life.

I am grateful for the knowledge that my health and my life are divinely created and divinely guided. I say, "Thank you" for the ability to replace any known or unknown fear I might have about my health with a pure and perfect faith in the Spiritual Truth.

And so I release this Truth, and all known and unknown fears that are not in alignment with this Truth, into the Law. There is no magic, just Principle at work in my life.

Yes! Complete!

Financial Freedom

God is unlimited in energy and in power. God is the source of all abundance and prosperity. Abundance and prosperity are simply God's energy manifested in financial currency and wealth. God makes this energy, abundance and prosperity available to every person who claims it. There is no separation from God's abundance based on race, gender, age, or any other human quality.

There is no checkpoint or gatekeeper standing between me and God. As a human manifestation of God I am a part of God and God is in all I am and all I do.

I am wealthy. I have the financial resources to cover all expenses and to provide for all my needs for my entire life. I use my wealth to provide support, encouragement and education to people who need it and to organizations that address issues and concerns I am passionate about. I love the feeling of security and stability that washes over me when I look at my bank balances, when I pay outstanding bills and when I donate to charities of my choice. I am a responsible steward of all money I receive and have more than enough to insure a safe and secure future for myself for as long as I live in human form.

For this I am grateful. With deep gratitude I realize my claim to the unlimited energy that forms as money and other resources is undeniable. This Truth is unquestionable and lives through me . . . now and forever more.

And So It Is.

For Employment and Health

Stop. Breathe. This air is provided by God. It is always present and available.

I breathe it in. It nourishes me and provides all I need to stay alive. I exhale and release all I have used and no longer need. I pass it on into the world to supply carbon dioxide for other elements of life.

This breathing in and breathing out is exactly how Spirit provides for me. Spirit is the everlasting breath. Spirit is the ever present source. Spirit is the coming and in and going out energy that supplies all I need. And It transforms within me to create the gifts, talents and services I share with the world.

I am intrinsically connected with Spirit. No separation. Spirit is in me, shows up as me, and works through me. My life is simply one breath after another ... breathing in the essential nature of God and breathing out all that no longer serves me or is perfectly designed to serve others.

I am 100% made in the spiritual likeness and image of God. I am provided for by Spirit and every need is met. I walk, step by step, through life expressing the love of God in all I do and say.

And so those experiences that show up as distractions to the Truth are simply temporary hooks into my human perception of limitation, lack, fear or pain but they are temporary and short-lived because I know the truth of me. And I know I have a long history of being guided and protect by Spirit. I know I have experienced miracles before and will experience miracles again. I know that I am completely dedicated to living a Spirit-filled life.

So I stand here, in this moment, claiming and affirming constant movement in the flow of the Universe. I claim and I find myself experiencing avalanches of prosperity and oceans of wellness. I am willing to replace fear, doubt and worry with faith, prayer and love.

I stand here now knowing the Spiritual Truth is that I do not need to beg or whine or bargain with God. No! It is my birthright to experience a life of joy with ease and grace. There is no test to pass and no paper to write. There is no mountain to climb. There is no penance to pay nor any punishment to survive. And there is no cross to bear. Spirit is all love, all the time and every creation of Spirit has an open door to the best life has to offer.

And so all that is required is clarity about what I want to experience and a deep belief that my desires are possible.

I have set an intention for a smooth and quick transition into a new joy. I meant to say job - but Spirit spoke the word joy. That is what I am demanding: Employment that is a joy. Coworkers, customers and vendors who are a joy to work with. A job that provides enough money to live a life filled with joy. Yes, this next joy in my life is assured.

And the right resources, the right people and the right healing are assured for me as well. Health and wellness for each person shows up differently so it is not possible to compare the abilities and conditions of any one person to another. But I know that my physical body has the prototype for its best health present in every cell. And I stand firmly, right here and right now, knowing that my intention for my health to support an independent and active lifestyle is promised.

I am deeply grateful for the love of God. It is this love that lets me say without any doubt that I and God are all one Presence.

And so I release this Word into Divine flow knowing that as I have thought and spoken each word the Universe simply took dictation and said, "OK, No problem ... I'm on it!"

God is good. And So It Is.

Joyful Anticipation

I am aware in this moment of the blessing of breath. God breathes Life into all of life.

My life begins with each breath.

I am grateful for the blessing of breath … of life … of opportunity … of possibility. Believing in the power of possibility is opening the door to my unlimited prosperity and joy. All I want is possible. Now.

I am grateful for God's offering of the world and my opportunity to create a life I choose.

So I go into this day with joyful anticipation of all the good there is to experience and share!

Amen … And So It Is!

Depressed, Hopeless and Lonely

I stand right here and now in faith. I am neither fooled nor distracted by the appearance of anything that is frustrating or frightening. I know that God is my Source and the Universe is always conspiring for my good.

Any brick walls and blocked doors are simply redirecting me toward my best and highest good. So I celebrate this day. I celebrate my life.

I notice my sadness, my loneliness and my fear. I accept that these are normal human reactions to temporary conditions. So I look them in the face and ask them, "What is mine to learn from you?" then let them go. Rumi says to greet emotions like they are houseguests: invite them in, treat them respectfully and then encourage them to leave when their time is up.

I do not fight my emotions I notice them, acknowledge them and then release them. I stand firmly in the knowing that this human experience is a gift and I am a gift to the world.

Grateful, I just release the pain, the frustration, the fear and the disbelief. I claim my perfect place in the Universe and pay attention to the signs that all is well.

As it is spoken; so it is done.

Relief from Pain

Health. Every breath in and every breath out is the reminder of health expressing unfettered. Health in its absolute is a constant breathing in of nourishment and life ... and the breathing out of all that's not needed and more life. The breath ... and the health ... are perfectly connected as the expression of God.

Peace. In the quiet of this moment I feel no worry, no need to analyze and no need to act. There is a perfect Peace in this moment that is simply a reminder of the Perfect Peace of God.

I am made of this same health and peace. There is no thing that has more power than perfect health and perfect peace in my life.

And so, in this moment I simply stand firm in the Truth that my health is God's health. Pain is a valuable signal designed to attract attention and so I am paying attention to that which is trying to be released. In fact, what is happening is I am right now releasing whatever physical and emotional and mental activity that is no longer in alignment with my best and highest good.

But this pain is just a temporary experience. It has no power over the eternal experience of life. It has no power over the full and total Truth of God; and so it can have no power over the full expression of life in, as and through me. This pain is simply an attention getter; it is an alarm or alert that now is the time to grow. Now is the time to acknowledge that which is out of alignment. Now is the time to release it, not cling to it.

My natural state is a state of health. I do not yield to the appearance of illness, weakness, pain or irritation. I do not yield to these human experiences because I know, and believe, in the power and presence of Perfection. I know this is a good experience disguised in a condition that appears to be difficult or bad. In the face of pain I scream, "Nonsense!" There can be nothing that is bad, except on its face. But the face is not the whole. So I cling to the whole and refuse to give the face of this situation my belief. I see it ... but I know it is just a part of a total story and that total story is good. I am good. God is good. And good is God.

So I relax into the knowingness that God is at work here, which means there is no need for worry or fear. There is no need for concern. I am in the hand and heart of God and so this pain reveals a hidden jewel. I am in the hand and heart of God so my doctor must be guided and directed by Spirit. I am in the hand and heart of God so there can be no other outcome than this pain releasing, retreating and revealing the Truth that now needs to be revealed in my life.

I am deeply grateful for my quick attention to the alerts of God. I am grateful I know my own Divinity and know my life is God's life. I am grateful that Truth, and only Truth always prevails.

These words are Truth and I release them now into the action of Universal Law.

And So It Is.

Weathering the Storms of Life

Dear God –

When the storms of life wash into my life it becomes obvious that I am unprepared to deal with them alone. I am grateful for the protection you provide by keeping me out of the path of the most destructive tornadoes.

I thank you too for reminding me that when the storms hit close to home it is an opportunity to refresh my resources and renew my commitment to the kind of preparation that will allow me to weather the unexpected storms that come into every person's life sooner or later.

Who am I to think I live in a storm-free zone, when I know there is a season for tornadoes, hurricanes, wild fires, tsunamis and other cleansing occurrences in every region of the world? I know there might be all kinds of storms: financial storms, relationship storms, career storms, family storms, self-esteem storms; and that certain types of storms can be anticipated in specific seasons of life.

When I am unprepared, these types of events can feel like disasters. But when I am prepared, they can be viewed as transitions and fresh starts.

My wish today, dear God, is to be renewed in my commitment to be prepared. My wish today, dear God, is to remember that being prepared requires me to do two things.

> First I must be in communion with you to be spiritually and emotionally ready for any storm that occurs ... with or without warning.

> And second, I must be in compliance with those physical things I can do to have access, on a moment's notice, to the tools, resources and people I need to survive the life storms I encounter.

Help me God to be both in communion and in compliance so the storms in my life are unable to demolish my life.

Thank you God for being my source of both strength and stability during the tornadoes that enter my life. And thank you for giving me the ability to protect myself from being devastated by storms big or small.

I am grateful to know that weather is temporary and God is permanent.

With Divine Guidance, support and love I do not fear the storm seasons in my life. I am fully prepared to survive each storm and find the fresh start that keeps me connect to You.

As it is spoken; so it is done.

Every Action is Guided

The Infinite Intelligence of the Universe is beyond description, beyond understanding and beyond limitation. All that has ever been known, all that is known now, and all that will ever be known is active in Divine Mind.

This Intelligence binds me to It. And I bind myself to It.

And so I know it is from Intelligence that my every action is guided. My choices are made by first tapping into this Intelligence. Everything I do today represents my reliance on the Intelligence that knows not only what to do, but when and how to do it.

I am grateful to know this Intelligence guides me and all of life.

I release, right now, anything and everything that is out of alignment with this Intelligence and make room for the Divine Activity of the Law to rule my life.

Blessed. And So It Is!

Wealth

I believe in the unlimited nature of the Universe. There is no limit to any energy of God, including the energy known as money, the energy known as safety and security, the energy known as joy, the energy known as love, and the energy known as freedom.

I am the physical manifestation of an idea that began in the Mind of God ... and so I am completely connected with all energies of God. There is nothing that can create a lasting separation between all that is God and all that is me.

So I am happy and grateful to receive a steady and never ending flow of money from expected and unexpected sources. My financial wealth allows me to live a life of joy and generosity. God is the source of all wealth and through me God encourages, challenges and supports many people on earth. I am a ready and willing vessel of wealth, accepting my riches and sharing my excess with people and programs that align with my passions.

I am grateful for the opportunity to experience financial freedom and to express love by funding those who need my support. I am grateful to live in an unlimited universe funded by a Divine Source of all things Good.

I release this prayer into Divine Law and allow it to work in me, as me and through me.

Yea and Amen.

Mortgage

Spirit has no form or shape. Spirit is not bound by time or space. But Spirit keeps the bodies of 7 billion people breathing and living all at the same time. And on top of that Spirit maintains the life of innumerable other beings and knows how to manage every cycle of life (morning to night, spring to fall, birth to death). There is no detail too small and no concept too large for Spirit to handle with Infinite Intelligence and in Divine Order.

This Divine Order and Infinite Intelligence is in my DNA and a part of my every breath.

I stand in the clarity that the process of securing a mortgage for my new home is guided and directed by Spirit. This is a God process in motion. Each change and shift is happening as a step toward my best and highest good.

I know this is an opportunity to practice faith and to release any old habits or false beliefs that no longer serve me.

I bless each "no" as completely as I bless each "yes" because I am sure there are no mistakes in God. I know the ease of moving from one lender to another in order to find the best rate and relationship is what is happening here. I know the grace of God is what is making each next step obvious and available.

I refuse to be distracted by any anxiety, any lack of confidence or any physical tiredness. I release all belief in being weary, afraid or impatient. Those are just old patterns and false beliefs that no longer apply to me.

The truth is this: I am ready for this new home. I am ready for this new loan. I am ready for the move. I am financially ready. I am emotionally ready. And I am physically ready. Old patterns and old hurts are now healed and have no power over me now. I am willing to take action, move forward and keep moving toward my best and highest good.

This house-buying adventure is being guided by a natural, spiritually grounded progression and cannot be tainted in any way by human condition past or present. I know, at the heart of it all, Spirit is reconfiguring every thing that needs to be reconfigured.

So I know this new home in this fabulous neighborhood – or something better – is mine. Securing the loan to finance the purchase is just one step in the process. And this process has been designed to work in my favor; so I know I will be approved by the right lender for the right amount of money in time to complete the contract on the right home for me.

I am most grateful for the predictability of Spirit. Universal Law does not pick favorites. It is always working. It never takes a vacation or turns its back. My request to secure the mortgage quickly and easily has been heard and is already done in Divine Mind.

So I deliberately step out of the lead and confidently follow God's footsteps.

And So It Is!

Moving Day

Divine Order: insuring that every season and every cycle falls into place. Joy: reflecting the fulfillment and peace of a life well lived. Wisdom: knowing what to do and how to do it. Divine Order. Joy. Wisdom. These are just three of the qualities of God that are always present.

These qualities are also present in me ... because I am one with God.

I walk, talk, think and act in a state of calm knowing that as I complete this move I experience the Wisdom of God present with me at all times. I complete each milestone step-by-step, allowing Divine Order to guide me.

This move is just one more piece of the puzzle falling into place. I have set an intention to live in joy ... and this new residence provides me with the perfect opportunity and the perfect environment to experience joy daily. Everything that is not in alignment with this joy is being removed from my life, right here and now!

I am so grateful for this exciting time in my life. It is so apparent that my prayers are being answered as I move from a place that does not align with my current vibration into a new residence that is more suitable to my joyful intentions. I am grateful for all the ways Spirit works in, as and through me to move me toward my best and highest good.

So I just release these words into the flow of Divine Activity.

And So It Is!

Health & Wholeness

What I know is absolutely True is that God is Perfect. God is the Perfect expression of life. God is Perfect health and wellness.

Because I have been made in the spiritual image and likeness of God I too express as Perfect health and wellness.

My health and my abundance are fully provided for. I believe in the perfect health of Spirit and know I am totally aligned with that. My body ages effortless and all systems remain healthy and strong.

I breathe easily. My heart and my lungs work together to circulate all I need for full energy and full life. I make healthy food choices and my entire gastric system works with ease to process the food and allow it to nourish my body.

I am healthy. Healthy is my natural state. I am able to dance and skate and be active. I am strong and alert and full of energy.

Spirit only knows health and wholeness and I am one with Spirit. There is nothing to fear; nothing to imagine and nothing to worry about. So I refuse to speak of worry. I turn my back on concern or possibility. I speak now of the health that exists and expands in my body.

My elbow, my heart, my lungs, my kidneys, my spleen, my entire gastrointestinal system, my nails ... in fact my entire physical body and all organs and systems within it work perfectly and in conjunction with each other to provide a healthy and strong container for my life!

I am so grateful for knowing that this is the Truth of my existence.

I release these words into the flow of Divine activity.

It is Done.

Trapped and Alone

The Truth of Life is evidenced every day by the breath. I breathe in deeply and the oxygen I need is right there. It fills my lungs and starts a chain reaction that feeds every part of my body. I exhale and everything my body no longer needs is pushed out to find its way of being of service to another creation.

It is this cycle of 'in and out' that reminds me the Universe knows exactly what it is doing. It never lets me down. It never fails to provides exactly what I need. It never looks away, takes a vacation or leaves me on my own to figure out what to breathe, how to breathe or when to breathe.

This is the Divine Nature of Perfection operating in, as and through all of creation. It is natural. It is easy. It is guaranteed.

My life is an example of Creation. My life is the manifestation of Creation. I don't need to know how it works but I am the example of It working. With every breath I take and every choice I make, God lives in me, as me and through me. God's life is my life and my life is God's.

So I speak this word for my Perfect life. I refuse to be distracted by appearances, old stories, or false beliefs. I trust completely in the Divine Order of the Universe. I know It is always operating for my best and highest good. I walk in complete faith that this challenge I now face is completely about presenting opportunities for me to redefine what I want to experience and reclaim who I want to be.

Right now is not a repeat of anything in the past. I am not trapped in a recurring pattern. This is not the movie Groundhog Day. This moment, this day, this week is simply what is happening in the present moment to birth tomorrow's Good.

This experience is neither a prank nor a prison. There are neither trick doors nor bars to be locked behind. This is simply the soil through which tomorrow's roses are being nurtured.

This is not a punishment of any kind. I am keeping my eyes open for the growth occurring here. There is always growth and only forward moving action in Spirit so there can only be growth and forward moving action being offered right now.

I must be ready for whatever challenges this current situation offers because Universal Law only provides me with the specific experiences I need to move to my next level of good. I am willing to consider that the answer to my prayers is being provided cleverly disguised as challenges and habits that are ready to be transformed.

So, beginning now, I claim this as a time for joyful expansion into new ways of being and a time to release any sense of contraction based on my old ways of being.

I open my mind, my heart and my arms to the guidance and support of God expressing in, as and through the dozens of people who care about me. I am willing to request and receive help not from a place of weakness or resentment but instead from a place of strength and entitlement. I am entitled to support because I am a part of the great Community of God.

I know, and believe with my entire being, that I am completely supported by the entire Universe. I have seen evidence of this time and time again. I know those examples were not exceptions but instead the simple manifestation of God's Good in physical form. God's Good is always present and so I open my mind, my heart and my arms to the Good right in front of me.

For this Good I am grateful. For God expressing in my life I am grateful. For life itself, I am deeply grateful.

I let go and allow God to do what God does best.

Yes! Complete!

For Love and Compassion

God, Spirit, the always present power is the source of all there is. God is the love planted as a tiny seed in every creation. Spirit is the compassion tucked into the corner of every heart.

I am a being of and from this source living in the human experience. Spirit is all I am every moment of every day.

The combination of love and compassion show up as patience in those times when the human me might prefer to be irritated or angry. This Truth is so deeply ingrained in me I have no doubt about it.

I am one with Spirit and all the qualities of God flourish in and through me. So I accept the divine love and never ending compassion I am. I recognize the way patience is an outpicturing of my infinite capacity for love and compassion. I see my core value of beauty guiding me to recognize the beauty in all of creation (including the people who place unreasonable demands upon me).

I recognize there is nothing I can do that is not of Spirit, so I see me responding to all requests as Spirit would respond. I see myself, right now, releasing the Christ Presence, the Buddha Nature, the love of God, in every conversation and every relationship I am involved in.

What great gratitude washes over me as I remember the power of the Spiritual Truth. I am grateful for Spirit living in and through me.

I release this Word into the Law knowing it is perfect. It is whole. It is done.

And So It Is.

Peace and Protection

Dear God,

Thank you for preparing a place of protection for me. Thank you for teaching me there is no shame in retreat for renewal.

I know I can turn away from those who would harm me and find a safe place where your Truth will protect me and provide the perspective and power I need to walk safely in the world.

Help me rely less on the illusion of security provided by alarm systems, cell phones and dialing 911. Help me recognize war and fighting are neither lasting protections nor paths to peace. Help me to recognize my daily opportunities to renew my safe place within.

And help me nurture that space so I can go there without hesitation and with full trust that protection and renewal are always available for me.

Let me be fully present and aware of the dangers that threaten my peace but fully trust in my ability to get myself safely to my secret, safe space within.

Thank you, God, for preparing a place of Divine Protection for me. You are the source of my peace. Grateful.

Amen.

Health Crisis

I know that God is always present. I know that life is always unfolding. I know that Divine Order is the truth of every moment.

My life reflects the perfectly unfolding nature of God.

Therefore, I stand in confidence knowing that life is expressing perfectly in this moment. I know that human conditions and circumstances do not define the true and essential nature of any person. I know that every change in condition is a step toward my best and highest good.

I refuse to be distracted by any diagnosis or any label because I know that every human experience is playing an important role in the expression of life. I am not afraid of any diagnosis or label because I know I am first and foremost a child of God. There is nothing that is truer than the fact that I am God expressing and God is always expressing perfectly.

So this experience of dis-ease is simply a temporary experience. I am not attached to it as right or wrong or good or bad. I know that I am, in every moment, able to choose how much power this has on my experience of life. And I have access to all the tools, resources, experts, mentors, supporters and friends I need to navigate this experience perfectly.

I am grateful for my belief in the Spiritual Truth. I am grateful that I do not have to understand everything that happens to have complete and total faith that it is all evolving into a perfect outcome. I am grateful for my life.

I trust Spirit to manifest the perfect outcome. I release. I let go.

As it is spoken; so it is done.

Loss of a Pet

Spirit. Love. Beauty. Allah. Joy. Peace. We have many names for God. But by any name, this Energy is without boundary and pure love.

Every part of me is filled with this boundary-less Energy and this pure Love.

This boundless energy and pure love is the limitless connection between me and my dog. No limitations the human mind can experience or imagine can separate the pure love we share. In the human experience of death, the physical body changes. It grows still and cold. It stops breathing. But the connection of love and the pure energy that is God energy cannot stop, cannot get cold, cannot end.

I know whenever I see my dog in my mind's eye I smile because I see her sitting at the bottom of a tree just waiting for her moment to chase the birds or squirrels hiding within. I am forever connected in love to this beloved creature. Nothing can change that. Nothing can take that away.

Thank you God for making the Truth so simple and so consistent. Thank you God for bringing love, in the form of my dog, into my life and into the world.

The power of this claim cannot be challenged as I release these words into the Law. It is done. It is so.

Amen.

Divine Right Action

There is only one Energy that exists in all things. That energy is the creator and the creation. That energy is wise and all knowing. That Energy I call God is always working toward good.

I am one with this amazing energy that demonstrates as wisdom and good works.

Because I am one with this energy of wisdom and knowledge there is no reason for me to question or doubt the outcome of my efforts. I am sure that Divine right action is happening in my life right now. I trust the wisdom of the Divine to guide my choices and guard my actions. Everything that is unfolding is unfolding perfectly, right now. And it is good.

I am so grateful for my understanding of the nature of God. I am so grateful that the only answer the Universe can give me is YES!

And so I release this into the river of the Law knowing that this claim is even now flowing into form and substance.

Amen.

Patience and Harmony

Every moment of every day is created and guided by Spirit. Everything happens just the way it is supposed to because God is in every thing, every action, every breath, every second, every creation, every decision and every thought.

Every creature, including myself, lives a life totally guided by this Spirit that is all and is in all, including me. My thoughts and my actions are divinely guided and have good purpose. And I am totally connected with every other human being (and every other creature) because we are all one in the mind and the soul of God.

I am responsible for my choices and my reactions. I choose to be grounded by Spirit as I act and react to each request made of me. When I do this I am patient. I am kind. I have no need to be right or to save the day. It is not mine to fix the problems created by others.

I can be a loving presence who serves our team and Spirit at the same time. I easily forgive myself, and all others, for actions that result in confusion or unintentional misunderstanding. I can be gentle with myself and others, even when I am in a leadership role.

I am so grateful for the knowledge that Spirit is able to do all things and that It works, every day, through me expressing as my best self in the world.

And so, I breathe in this Truth and call it True. I accept it and remind myself I am already, in this new breath, walking a new Path. It is done.

And So It Is!

Patience and Compassion

God ... Spirit ... the always present power and source of all there is. God is the love planted as a tiny seed in every creation. Spirit is the compassion tucked into the corner of every heart.

I am a being created of and from this source ... living in the human experience.

I call on the spiritual combination of love and compassion to show up as patience when I might prefer to be irritated or angry.

I deny the power of anger, frustration, irritation or resentment to control my actions or beliefs. I am one with Spirit and all the qualities of God flourish in and through me.

So I accept the divine love and never ending compassion I am. I recognize the way patience is an outpicturing of my infinite capacity for love and compassion. I welcome the opportunity to see beauty in all of creation, including people who irritate me or place unreasonable demands upon me. I recognize irritation and unreasonable are my perception and I can change my perception and my reaction at any time.

I recognize there is nothing I can do that is not of Spirit, so I choose to respond to all requests as Spirit would respond.

I can set clear boundaries, communicate calmly and act from love in every conversation and every relationship I am involved in.

What great gratitude washes over me as I remember the power of the Spiritual Truth. I am thankful for Spirit's presence in me every moment of every day.

So I release this Word into the Divine activity of the Law knowing it is perfect; it is whole and it is done.

And So It Is.

The Energy of Money

God is abundance, prosperity, financial freedom and joy. Now that is the TRUTH.

And I am made of God so I AM abundance, prosperity, financial freedom and joy.

ANY thing that looks different from abundance, prosperity, financial freedom and joy is not more powerful nor more present nor more true than God.

Any fear, worry or doubt about financial self-sufficiency is a LIE ... a downright human, stupid, fear-based LIE and I put it down RIGHT NOW!

What I know is that in the joy and the love and the abundance of my life: bank statements, financial obligations and unexpected bills are TOTALLY COVERED by the joy and the love and the abundance of God.

So I refuse to argue with logic. Instead I put my total and complete faithfulness to love and law into action and I know my life right now is filling up with the money required to meet every obligation, every desire and every opportunity placed in my life.

I express life as the power and presence of God in all ways ... and that includes the form and energy of money. This is a DONE DEAL!

So with deep gratitude I release this knowing into the already active Law,

Yes! Complete!

Pain

Health. Every breath in and every breath out is the reminder of health expressing unfettered. Health in its absolute is a constant breathing in of nourishment and life ... and the breathing out of all that's not needed and more life. The breath ... and the health ... are perfectly connected as the expression of God.

Peace. In the quiet of this moment I feel no worry, no need to analyze and no need to act. There is a perfect Peace in this moment that is simply a reminder of the Perfect Peace of God.

I am made of this same health and peace. There is no thing that has more power than perfect health and perfect peace in my life.

And so, in this moment I simply stand firm in the Truth of my health. My health is God's health. Pain is a valuable signal designed to attract attention so I am paying attention to that which is trying to be released. In fact, I am right now releasing whatever physical and emotional and mental activity that is no longer in alignment with my best and highest good.

I know pain is just a temporary experience. It has no power over the eternal experience of life. It has no power over the full and total Truth of God. And so it can have no power over the full expression of life in, as and through me.

This pain is simply an attention getter and an alarm or alert that now is the time to grow. Now is the time to acknowledge that which is out of alignment. Now is the time to release it, not cling to it.

My natural state is a state of health. I do not yield to the appearance of illness, weakness, pain or irritation. I do not yield to these human experiences because I know, and believe, in the power and presence of Perfection. I know this is a good experience disguised in a condition that appears to be difficult or bad.

In the face of pain I scream, "Rubbish!" There can be nothing that is bad, except on its face. But the face is not the whole. So I cling to the whole and refuse to give the face of this situation my belief. I see it ... but I know it is just a tiny part of a total story and that total story is about good. I am good. God is good. And good is God.

So I relax into the knowingness that God is at work here which means there is no need for worry or fear. There is no need for concern. I am in the hand and heart of God and so this pain reveals a hidden jewel. I am in the hand and heart of God so my doctor must be guided and directed by Spirit. I am in the hand and heart of God so there can be no other outcome than this pain releasing, retreating and revealing the Truth that now needs to be revealed.

I am deeply grateful I know my Divinity and know my life is God's life. I am grateful that Truth, and only Truth always prevails.

These words are Truth and I release them now into the action of Universal Law.

And So It is.

Health and Wholeness

There is only health and wholeness in God.

And so I know my true essential nature is also health and wholeness.

My health and life are held in the loving hand of Spirit. I refuse to be distracted by the appearance of disability or weakness. I release any attachment my human self may have to old stories and past beliefs about stroke. And I replace those old stories and past beliefs with the absolute knowledge of the power and the presence of God in this situation.

I know that every medical professional related in any way to my care is guided by Divine Wisdom. I know that every person who provides care for me is guided, guarded and directed by Divine right action and is completely surrounded by Love.

I am grateful that my deepest desires and strongest beliefs are heard now by the Universe and Divine Mind has already said YES.

And so I get out of the way. I give this to God.

And So It Is!

Incubation not Depression

Spirit is Joy. Spirit is Divine Order. Spirit is Wisdom operating always for Good.

My essential nature is Joy. My life is always unfolding in Divine Order. And I am Wisdom operating always for Good. I am Spirit expressing in every aspect of my life. This is my natural state of being.

Because I can see and celebrate joy in, and for, others I know my Oneness with God is not broken. There is no question that my life and my work are Divinely guided.

So my intention now is to see and celebrate both mental clarity and deep understanding of Spirit's Highest Vision for ME. Even when I can't see it clearly, I know that Joy is emerging from the inner recesses of my soul just like the spring plants are emerging from the protection of the winter soil.

I know that Principle is not bound by precedent. Spirit is always creating something new. So even though these feelings and behaviors look and feel very much like what I have labeled depression in the past, I am willing to consider that it might be incubation.

Depression is grounded in what is dying or missing. Incubation is grounded in what is birthing and growing. They look the same in human expression but are complete opposites in their spiritual and mental foundation.

My vision for the next stage of my life requires me to release the old and take on the new. I am simply emptying the old and sitting in the in-between time. I choose now to fill the empty spaces in my mind and heart with the vision I know continues to unfold: I am a joy-filled example of service and prosperity!

I have set a new Cause into Motion and it is being transferred cell by cell into my experience of life. I know that Spirit's Vision and my vision are aligned at all times. So I remind myself of my vision every chance I get. And whenever I hear my human mind trying to label the emptiness as bad or dangerous or inappropriate, I say, "Cancel, cancel! Delete, delete! I'm whole; I'm perfect; I am complete!"

My life is like a field of Texas wildflowers that month after month look like well-maintained weeds on the side of the road. And then one day, you drive by there are beautiful, bright Bluebonnets blooming everywhere announcing the return of spring.

The Bluebonnet blooms anew because it has taken in all the nutrients it needs in the darkness and the silence of winter. But it never doubts it purpose and it never doubts the season of change is ordained. When it is dark and underground, it simply deepens its roots and grows. Perhaps it imagines that moment when it gets to break through the soil and feel the sun again, but it recognizes the season of darkness is preparing it to bloom again and serve as the beautiful backdrop for thousands of photographs bringing joy to the lives of countless people.

Throughout the winter the field of Bluebonnets is maintained by conscious effort. The grass around them is cut. The rain waters the ground. Additional water is provided if there isn't enough rain to deeply nourish the plant. There is attention being paid to what is required for each Bluebonnet to bloom again.

There is no worry about it not blooming, just consistent service to the image of a field of beautiful, Bluebonnets returning in the spring. I choose to be the caretaker to my image of myself as a joy-filled example of service and prosperity!

I know how Spiritual Law works. I know that everything that is happening is always happening to move me closer to my best and highest good. So I claim this time as a passage from who I have been to who I am becoming.

I am so grateful to know this is not idle hope; it is promised renewal. This is not wishful thinking; it is life unfolding. This is not punishment; it is preparation. This is not depression; it is deepening.

So I release my self into the Limitless Self of Spirit.

As it is spoken; so it is done.

Rebirth (Happy Birthday Prayer)

God is an always present, always renewing energy. There is no birth in God. There is no death in God. There is no beginning in God. There is no end in God. There is only a constantly renewing, recycling, and refreshing energy of Life.

The energy of Life doesn't end with each season. Life as winter flows into spring; spring into summer; summer into autumn and autumn back into winter. It is all Life renewing Itself, reinventing Itself, recharging Itself and releasing Itself into each greater expression.

This infinite energy of Life I call God is eternal and immortal and it is expressing right now as my life and the life of all of Creation.

So today I awake into a re-birth. I am daily born again into the freshness of Life. I am daily releasing my attachment to what is past and that which no longer serves me so I can be open to the fullness of my birthright.

On this day I say yes to the Perfection of Spirit rushing in to experience and express something new.

I say yes to the Power of Spirit transporting me toward my best and highest Good. I am always growing, always expanding, always exploring and always receiving my Good. And, as Emma Curtis Hopkins reminds me, "My Good is my God."

I say yes to the Presence of Spirit breathing every breath and thinking every thought I call my own. I am a living example of humanity re-birthing into its spiritual magnificence. I accept today as an opportunity to celebrate all experiences in my life even as I demonstrate my willingness to shed the bright past for a brilliant future.

I am so grateful that with every inhale I am reminded that my energy comes from an Infinite Source. I am grateful that with each exhale I am assured anything that no longer serves me is easily released. I am grateful for the cycles of life for I understand cycles connect to each other in a never-ending continuation of Divine Expression.

So it is with clarity and conviction that I release these words into Universal Law and accept my place in the Infinite flow of ever expanding Life.

And So It Is!

Prayer Poems

"It doesn't matter how you pray--with your head bowed in silence, or crying out in grief, or dancing. Churches are good for prayer, but so are garages and cars and mountains and showers and dance floors."

Anne Lamott

Grounded by Gratitude

As the world spins around me
out of control
doing it's thing
on it's own schedule
meeting its own needs
I wonder
What is my place?
Where am I going?
How can I be happy when everything is moving so fast?
But happiness is not hard.
I just stop and say, "Thank you God"
    Thank you for another day.
    Thank you for an opportunity to make a difference.
    Thank you for friends.
    Thank you for work.
    Thank you for family.
    Thank you for food.
    Thank you for love.
    Thank you for growth.
    Thank you for good health.
    Thank you God for all I have, all I am and all I experience.
The world can spin but it doesn't make me dizzy.
When I am grounded by gratitude.

Today's Faith

faith.
keep the faith.
now is not the time for doubt.
now is not the time for fear.
just have faith.
for one more day.
today.
faith.

Courageous

in the line of fire
the flames advance
you feel the heat
you smell the scent
but nothing in you retreats.

god speaks in your voice
and directs every move
doing that which you cannot
knowing that which you know not.

with gratitude you credit faith
when the world calls you courageous.

i am

i am calm in a raging storm
i am peace in times of war
i am generosity in time of limitations
i am joy in times of great sadness
i am beauty in times of devastation
i am love in times of fear
in all times
i am of God
i am

The Release

If you gave up your story, who would you be?

If you gave up your belief that you are damaged and broken, what would you do?

If you gave up being afraid to be successful, what would unfold?

If you gave up the lie that other people know more than you, how would that change your relationships?

If you gave up waiting for a better future, what would you do differently today?

If you gave up who you were in the past, who could you be now?

If you gave up your weaknesses, where would your strengths take you?

If you gave up your attachment to failure, what would success look like?

If you gave up your pain, what would you fill your heart with?

If you gave up the goal of perfection, how much more might you accomplish?

If you gave up regrets, what would you think about yourself?

If you gave up your Dad's limitations, what goals would you set?

If you gave up your Mom's fears, what would you try?

If you gave up hiding from commitment, what risks would you take?

If you gave up the false belief that it's too late to change, what new future would you create?

If you gave up your doubts that you are loved by God, what would you ask for or create in your life?

Mirror, Mirror on the Wall

Look in the mirror and say, "I am good."
Look in the mirror and say, "I am love."
Look in the mirror and say, "My life matters."
Look in the mirror and say, "I love you."
Look in the mirror and say, "Thank you God."

more like a calling than a controlling

it is more like a calling
than a controlling.
> i am following the voice of Spirit.
> i am knowing.
> i am blowing through the barriers
> ignoring all the carriers
> of doubt and fear
> and accepting my path.

this is more a calling
than a controlling.
> i know I am not in charge
> i know that life is a gift to explore
> and everything i need
> is already in my core
> my core beliefs
> my core talents
> have been perfectly configured
> for Life Itself to
> experience humanity through me

So this is more a calling
than a controlling
> i accept this path
> i choose to walk it
> i choose to talk it
> i choose to experience it
> i choose to share it
> i choose to know it
> i choose to say yes

For this is more a calling than a controlling.

it's my life

I turn within
again.
and know my humanity.
the fear.
the disbelief.
the pain.
the uncertainty.
my ego is strong
and silent
and patient
awaiting its
opportunity
to control my life.

I turn within
again.
and know my divinity.
the peace.
the joy.
the confidence.
the certainty.
my spirit is strong
and silent
and patient
allowing me
to choose
what I want to call to Life.

why?

why?
we ask this question knowing
it is not our right
to know
it is only our right
to live
and experience
>   joy and pain
>   happiness and sadness
>   love and hate
>   ups and downs
there are lessons for us all
in each crisis we face
a gift for our heart or our soul.
so ask not why
but instead as what.
what lessons am i here to learn?
what growth am I here to attain?
remind yourself that all is perfect
in your life.
your life is god's work
a universal plan
based only on love.
and it's all good.

Choose Carefully

Life is a precious gift.
And time is short.
We all make mistakes.
We all have fears.
We all have dreams.

The first challenge is making the choice
to grow
and to serve.

The second challenge is
to take responsibility
for our choices.

Life is a precious gift
And time is short.

So choose quickly
and carefully.

To the Mother I Never Met

How can I thank you for dreaming me into existence?
You survived the Maafa for me.
You learned English so I could speak.
You picked cotton for me.
You loved the children created from rape so I could live.
You worked hard for me.
You made food from scraps so I could eat.
You endured lynching and Jim Crow for me.
You bowed your head so I could lift mine.
Now I live in a world with opportunity you could never have imagined.
I love you.
I am grateful for you.
Thank you.

Today I Say Yes

Today I say yes.
> Yes, to completing the old
> Yes, to entering the new
> Yes, to being of service
> Yes, to being in love with life

Today I say yes to Spirit's guidance
Today is a fresh start
> a new beginning
> a new lease on life

Today is an opportunity
> to change
> to grow
> to serve
> to love

Today is a beautiful day
Today is now
Today is for right action
Today is before me. Waiting.
Today I say yes!

Guide Me

Dear God,
I am grateful for all that I have.
And all I am.

Provide for me all I need.
Help me be love in words and actions.
Guide me in giving and sharing all that you are.
Show me the way to be an example of you.
Give me energy and health and wealth
So I can do what I came to do.

Live in the name of Love
Laugh in the name of Love
Learn in the name of Love
Lead in the name of Love

I love you and I love that you are me
I love that together we are One
Inseparable expression of Love

the healing

cry with me.
heal your soul.
release shame and blame.
forgive

be with me.
shed your fears.
look toward tomorrow.
hope

read with me.
seek your solution.
see your potential.
learn

pray with me.
release your questions.
count all your blessings.
believe

breathe with me.
find your center.
follow your guidance.
know

reach with me.
set your goals.
explore the unknown.
dream

talk with me.
tell your story.
practice compassion.
share

walk with me.
shape your future.
trust in divine law.
accept

love with me.
free your heart.
look in my eyes.
trust

search with me.
open your mind.
be the unfolding.
grow

climb with me.
smash your doubts.
ignore past boundaries.
stretch

play with me.
share your joy.
inspire great laughter.
smile

stand with me.
show your strength.
do more good than harm.
live

serve with me.
do your best.
be an example.
give

dance with me.
feel your bliss.
show your true colors.
create

rise with me.
live your dream.
break the old cycle.
change

flow with me.
honor your spirit.
fulfill your life mission.
love

fly with me.
change your mood.
transform your pain.
soar

Only Good Things to Say

I have not forgotten
    the bad days
    the mad days
    the mean and hateful ways
I have not forgotten
    the threats
    the accusations
    the lies or the betrayals
I have not forgotten but I have forgiven
You
And myself

I have not forgotten the pain, the fear or the failure
But when I speak of our relationship I don't share those things
And I don't let them take up more space in my heart than
The lessons I learned from you about
    sharing
    confidence
    family
    pride
    creativity
    sharing
    receiving
    learning
    laughter
    and love.

I was blessed by our friendship
I was blessed by our love
I was blessed by our trials
And I have been blessed by our separation

I only wish you happiness and peace of mind.

I only wish you inner peace.
I am grateful for the good things that came from our experience together.
I only have good things to say.

The Whole Me

no sharp edges
just curving lines
in constant motion
weaving in and out
of the traffic of life

that's me —
in 5 colors —
some earth
some bright
some separation
some overlap

confusing
if you focus on one part
too long

inspiring
if you step back and notice
the flow

no sharp edges
only bends in the road
no wrong answers
just adventures to unfold
separate paths connecting
and converging as one

when I let
the whole me
be

Spirit Help Me

I want to break the chains that bind me
I want to heal the pains that hurt me
i know the answer is in praying
Spirit, help me know the truth.

I want to break the chains that bind me
I want to heal the pains that hurt me
I know the answer is believing
Spirit, help me walk in faith

I want to break the chains that bind me
I want to heal the pains that hurt me
I know the answer is in healing
Spirit, help me heal my heart

I want to break the chains that bind me
I want to heal the pains that hurt me
I know the answer is forgiveness
Spirit, help me let things go

I want to break the chains that bind me
I want to heal the pains that hurt me
I know the answer is in giving
Spirit, help me share with joy

I want to break the chains that bind me
I want to heal the pains that hurt me
I know the answer is in pure love
Spirit, help me be the gift

I want to break the chains that bind me
I want to heal the pains that hurt me
I know the answer is in being
Spirit, help me act from peace

surrender is the path to serenity

when we surrender to what is
when we walk in our spiritual truth
when we accept our own humanity
when we allow our emotions to flow
we are walking the path of serenity
we are living in the land of paradise
we are experiencing heaven on earth
we are expressing our limitless potential

Release

Everything toxic is gone.
Everything toxic is gone.

I breath in God and all good.
When I breathe out I release fear.

It is so exciting to be successful!
It is so exciting to be wealthy!
It is so exciting to be loved!

The way is clear. There are
No blocks to prosperity.
No blocks to joy.

Business is getting better every day.
My life is wonderful in every way.

Everything toxic is gone.
Everything toxic is gone.

A Prayer for Action

Stop Wishing.
Start Knowing.
Stop Hoping.
Start Doing.
Stop Blaming.
Start Loving.
Stop Complaining.
Start Changing.
Only I can choose
How I show up in the world.

Some Day

There is no "some day"
There is only "now"

Every Day

You can change the world.
You DO change the world.
Every Day.

What will you be a catalyst for
TODAY?

Trust

It is not enough to accept an idea...
It cannot manifest until you trust it as real.
Until you behave as if it is the truth it cannot live.

It is not enough to tolerate a person
He cannot share with you his unique gifts and talents until you
trust he is your equal

Until you welcome her as you would welcome your twin she
cannot reveal her essence.

So do not pretend to love or believe.
Demonstrate your faith by your actions.

Show me what you believe and who you love
By what, and who, you trust.

Grateful

Grateful for another day!
Grateful for my health, my life, my friends, my talent, my knowledge of the Spiritual Truth.
Grateful for every opportunity to experience life.
Grateful I am.

I am overflowing with blessings.
I am pure potentiality expressing as a Divine (and Divinely guided) human spirit.
I am grateful.
I am grateful.
I am grateful!
And so It Is!

wi-fi God

my God
is a wi-fi God

in every space
all over the place
God's in the air
just everywhere

my God
is a wi-fi God

no need
for a cord
or a
plug
I'm tapped in
I'm pumped up
connected
selected
and ALWAYS protected

my God
is a wi-fi God

with a triune network
beyond compare
I'm checking in
I'm hooking up

I'm reaching out
to the energy of God.

Going Through and Growing Up

Growing up is hard to do.
So is growing through.

Challenges appear
Fear arrives
Getting stuck is common.

But change is life
So you adapt
And look for the good
And trust.

So instead of simply
going through
I am growing through
and growing up.

one with the infinite

I am ready
I am willing
I am excited

I am on fire
with love and light
with wisdom and wealth
with joy
with peace
with deep gratitude

I am one with Infinite Spirit
I am one with Infinite Source
I am one divine emanation of God
walking this earth
at this time
in human form
on purpose

Just a Little Reminder

Keep your head up
and your eyes on the future.

You are
in the right place
at the right time
having an experience of life
designed to teach and grow you.

Keep your head up
and your eyes on the future

You are
having an experience of life
designed to show others
life is not always easy
but life is never hopeless.

Keep your head up
and your eyes on the future

You are
having an experience of life
designed to show others
life is a shiny star
full of moments of joy

Keep your head up
and your eyes on the future

You are
having an experience of life
designed to remind us

no pain (and no joy)
is permanent.

Keep your head up
and your eyes on the future

You are
having an experience of life
but your experience today
is not all of who you are.

Keep your head up
and your eyes on the future

Live fully today
in gratitude
then take
one step at a time
toward tomorrow.

amicably divorced

it matters little to me what others think about
the books I've written
the places I've been
the people I know

what i want to be known for is
kindness
compassion
service
growth

i stand for
love in action
bringing people together
growing a bigger pie
(and a better world)

if along the way
i make a name for myself
that is collateral damage:
important to notice but
nothing to be distracted by

the spotlight has always been on
showing people what god looks like
in human form
and helping them see and be
their own divinity

so stuff i have done
is not who i am
i am neither embarrassed

nor impressed
by my achievements

i appreciate my past experiences
as my path of becoming
but think of me as
amicably divorced from yesterday's joys (and pains)

i am happily married to now
and tomorrow.

Choose Joy

Perfect.
Every second of every day is perfect.
You are perfect.
Your life is perfectly unfolding.
Breathe that in.
Release your fear.
Denounce your judgment.
Forgive your past.
Remember your birthright.
And choose joy.

reinvention

retreat within
relax my mind
redirect my energy
reinvent my life

Let Me Walk in Faith

Today, please help me focus on solutions not problems.

Today, help me forgive anyone I need to forgive (including myself).

Today, help me align what I know (about faith, joy and inner peace) with my every action.

Today, please let me walk in faith.

Let Me Be Love

Help me be (not just do).
Help me be kind and respectful.
Help me be patient and compassionate.
Help me see the good in people.
Help me be love.

ready to go forward

i am ready to go forward
i am ready for change
i am ready for my future
i am ready for the next phase
i am ready to serve
i am ready to be my i am
i am ready to love
i am ready to smile
i am ready to glow
i am ready to teach
i am ready to speak
i am ready to listen
i am ready to help
i am ready to guide
i am ready to meet
i am ready to learn
i am ready to grow
i am ready to flow
i am ready to go forward
guided by spirit
now

Nothing is Lost

Items lost, but not stolen.
Items left, but not forgotten.
Wrong address?
Turn left and walk 5 blocks in the other direction.

Survival is not the question.
Alternatives are available.
Replacements are provided.
Mid-course corrections are right on time.

So stay calm. Choose joy.
And don't forget that which is most important to you.
Because what is hidden from view is not necessarily gone.

Laugh at yourself because all is as it should be.
Revealed ... at the right time.

Just a Matter of Time

just a matter of time
it is just a matter of time
before i bloom into my best self
and since time is relative . . .
why not do it today?

Never Ready

Are you ever ready?
Never!
To say goodbye seems much too final.
You always wish you had time for
      one more hug
      one more joke
      one more history lesson
      one more email
      one more apology
      one more 'I Love You."
      one more phone call
One more day, hour or minute to enjoy each other and
To share life.

Are you ever ready?
Never!
To say goodbye seems much too final.
For no one dies completely when those who love him
      tell his story
      follow his example
      learn from his mistakes
      celebrate his successes
      honor his values
      respect his experiences
Remember the good times and
Appreciate the miracle of his life

Are you ever ready?
Never!

To say goodbye seems much too final.
So say "good life" instead.

Fare Well, My Brother

Your death is about loss

> Loss of life. Loss of time together. Loss of opportunities to laugh and love. Loss of a good man.

But your death is also about joy

> Joy from being who you are and walking in your truth. Joy from travel and exploring the world. Joy from art. Joy from being good and also doing good.

Your death is not the end

> There is no end to you. There is no end to the you you shared with each of us. We may say goodbye to the physical body you used to navigate this world but we can never release your spirit. You – your spirit – is woven into each one of us in immutable ways.

So while others say farewell and goodbye, my greeting to you today is, "Fare Well, my brother."

Your spirit soars on this new journey.

> And as much as you love to travel I imagine you shifting into a mode of curiosity and discovery as you explore your new home.

Your spirit soars on this new journey

> Because you have ascended to a place where there are no labels, no biases and there is no judgment.

Your spirit soars on this new journey

> And our spirits rise up to try to meet yours, knowing that our highest reach barely scrapes your lowest thought ... which means you have to be happier, healthier and more at peace than any one of us could ever imagine.

You will fare well on this exciting journey, my brother, because your years on earth have simply been the preparation for the next phase of your life.

Fare well. Travel safely. Know you are loved.

truly

blessed. truly blessed.
yes.
grateful. truly grateful.
now.
loved. truly loved.
forever.

help me today

help me today to
honor the good / honor the god
in all I do
in all I say
in all I think
in all I hope for

Infinite. Without Limit

I am infinite. Without limit.
I am not locked in a room
defined by ego or fear.
There is no room.
There are no walls.
My spirit
is your spirit
is our spirit
is all Spirit
expressing
without boundaries man made.
No room I create
is large enough to hold
the me that I am.
There is no room.
There are no walls.
I am infinite. Without limit.

Return to the Forever Soul

Return to the Forever Soul
Back to the basics.
Creating and keeping simple ritual
to stay on track
to maintain focus
to truly BE.

It would be easy to get caught up in doing;
but that's when life gets
confusing.
inconsistent.
crazy.

Returning to the basics is
a return to right mind
a return to God
a return to love
a return to wholeness

a return to the Forever Soul.

A Blessing

May your needs all be met
May your dreams be exceeded
May your joy be unending
Doctors never be needed
May you live a life long with no pain and no sorrow
May each day be so perfect you don't need a tomorrow.
May you love and be loved without limitation
May you know you are blessed with Supreme inspiration
For the life that you lead is Divinely protected
You are guided and guarded by a spiritual message
Know each step that you take and each day you continue
Are the notes for the song that is uniquely within you.

the answer

breathe.
breathe again.
wait.

breathe.
breathe again.
listen.

breathe.
breathe again.
smile.

breathe.
breathe again.
repeat

meditation is practice

practice helps
practice accepts
practice challenges
practice rewards

no problem meditating
 because every day is simply practice
because there is no goal beyond practice
because there are no mistakes; there's just practice
because there's no need for do-overs; just practice

just breathe.
just be.
just practice.
no problem.

i am

i am calm in a raging storm
i am peace in times of war
i am generosity in time of limitation
i am joy in times of great sadness
i am beauty in times of devastation
i am love in times of fear

in all times
i am the I AM

Transformation

I am not in charge of this transformation.
I know it is happening for a reason.
I know it is morphing me into someone better and different.
but I have no idea who that will be.

I can't figure out what's wrong because
there really isn't anything wrong.
I just don't like feeling like
I'm not in control or
I'm not creating my future.

So . . . like so many people before me
I must remember
when the caterpillar is in the cocoon
he doesn't know what's going on around him.
and he doesn't know what he is becoming.

But he also doesn't fight nature.
And he blooms into a beautiful butterfly
he never would have chosen to become ...
because it didn't look
like anything
or anyone
he had ever been before.

My job
is to be consciously thankful
for the good right in front of me
as many times a day as it takes
to keep me from
freaking out.

And if I can do that

- and mean it –
today will be happy.

And I will look back 5 years
or 10 years from now
and see exactly what was being birthed
during
this
darkness.

Ready to Begin. Again.

It is time to Begin. Again.
Now is a great time to Begin. Again.
Now is the Best time to Begin. Again.
OK, Spirit – it's you and me; let's Begin. Again.
Begin. Again.

Begin Again

born anew
a rebirth
taking all I know and creating a new beginning.

ascending
from doing spiritual practice
to being spiritual practice.

rising
from believing in Spirit
to living in Spirit.

every day as I walk with Spirit
I notice when the corners turn into curves
the darkness transforms into light
and the path is all Good all God.

i am Divinely directed
to choose my best and highest Good.

so i choose to
begin again
in all things
in all ways
in each present moment.

Shape Shifting

That me from yesterday is gone.
Today I start afresh.

Who do I want to be in this life?
How do I want to serve?
What do I want to do?
Where do I want to go?
How can I make a positive difference?
What do I want to learn?
What do I want to acquire?
What do I want to release?

If I remember that others meet God
through my words and actions
how does that change my choices?

That me from yesterday fades
and every morning I start afresh
and shape shift into
a new expression
of Love.

i am a beneficial presence

i am a beneficial presence.
i am a beneficial presence.
i am a beneficial presence.
i am a beneficial presence.

i am a beneficial presence.
really.
yes.
absolutely.
it's true.

all is well

breathe.
relax.
speak from your God center
and all will be well.

no reason to fear

I'm with you
just trust me
I'll make the
path clear

I'm with you
don't worry
no reason
to fear

Easter Sunday (Resurrection)

I stand in this place of
assuredness ...
knowing Your Divinity
is alive in me.

I stand in this moment of
eternality ...
knowing Your Perfection
breathes life into me.

I stand on this platform of
peace ...
knowing Your Wisdom
directs right action through me.

I stand for the truth of
Love ...
knowing Your Essence
transforms every cell in me.

I am the human expression of the Divine.
Reborn.
Renewed.
Resurrected.

Life and Death are One

God is infinite. eternal. changeless. always evolving. ever expanding.
Man is God in human form. So the essence of Man is infinite. eternal. changeless. always evolving. ever expanding.

Human form is what comes then goes. starts then stops. appears then gives way.

Knowing this, it becomes clear that
Life can only be lived fully when
Birth and death are viewed in perspective.
When birth and death are understood as the myth
That perfectly satisfies the human brain's need
To define and understand its experience of life.

No need to fear death. Welcome the change.
Consider it a rite of passage.
Like becoming a teenager. Or turning 21.
Becoming a parent. Graduating from college.
Buying your first car without your parent's help.
Being promoted into a job you're not quite sure you can handle.

By now, the unknown is an old friend you have met so many times before.

Death is simply a change.
A shift in perspective.
A new experience.
Welcome it.
Even when you don't seek it.
Or expect it.

When searching for the meaning of life
When filled with the busyness of fulfilling others' desires or
needs
When doubting my own knowledge or intuition
When caught in the maze of forgotten Truth
I feel lost and alone.
Confused and empty.
Sad and afraid.

I cannot die into peace when I have only lived in its opposite.
I cannot die into joy when I have felt nothing but pain.
I cannot die into love when I have feasted on a constant diet of
fear.
So it is no surprise I am afraid to die
Because I have not bathed in the light of Love or
Walked on the ground of Wisdom.

When choosing to follow my inner-most guidance
When knowing my journey is unique and can only be walked by
me
When remembering "It is my Father's good pleasure to give me
the Kingdom"
I feel alert and alive.
Connected and powerful.
Joyous and wise.

I cannot live without a daily diet of gratitude.
I cannot live without sharing my passion.
I cannot live without leaving a legacy of love.

So it is no surprise that I know how to die
Because I know how to live.
And I know who I am.

I am

Love
Joy
Wisdom
Order
Beauty
Balance and
Peace
I am
Power
Health
Freedom
Abundance
Prosperity
Intelligence
Creativity
Energy
Right Action and
Well Being

I am the Begotten Child, not the forgotten child.

God is infinite. eternal. changeless. always evolving. ever
expanding.
Man is God in human form. So the essence of Man is infinite.
eternal. changeless. always evolving. ever expanding.

Human form is what comes then goes. starts then stops. appears
then gives way.

Knowing this, it becomes clear that
Life can only be lived fully when
Birth and death are viewed in perspective.
When birth and death are understood as the myth
That perfectly satisfies the human brain's need
To define and understand its experience of life.

Today I Say Yes

Today I say yes.
    Yes, to completing the old
    Yes, to entering the new
    yes, to being of service
    Yes, to being in love with life

Today I say yes to Spirit's guidance.

Today is
a fresh start
a new beginning
a new lease on life

Today is an opportunity
to change
to grow
to serve
to love

Today is a beautiful day.
Today is now.
Today is for right action.
Today is before me.
Waiting.

So today
I say yes.

The World Does Not Need to Change

The world does not need to change
for me to be happy
for me to live in
or from
joy

bliss

floating
above the humanosphere

balanced
by the godmosphere

no need
no want
just bliss

unforgiveness removed

i can feel my heart beating in my chest.
no alarm.
no issue.
just beating ... life.

beating strongly and surely
    as if the unforgiveness removed
    and the no longer needed released
    opened up space
    to beat
    with glorious strength
    and great abandon

i can feel my heart beating in my chest.
no alarm.
no issue.
just beating ... love.

making more room for god

i am making more room for god
in my life through my spiritual practice

i am making more room for god
in the world through the work i do

i am making more room for god
in the universe through my life and my example

making more room for god
is my ever expanding role in the world
and it begins
within

i am willing to change
i am willing to grow
i am willing to listen
i am willing to share
i am willing to hope
i am willing to study
i am willing to dance
i am willing to help
i am willing to feel
i am willing to learn
i am willing to teach
i am willing to expand

i am willing to make more room for god
for god is all there is

essential nature

Looking deep within
I am reminded
of my deep, delicious
essential nature.

timeless.
all love.
wisdom
joy.

i am the peace that God is.
I am the I AM
showing up and expressing
Life.

Be Here Now

Step. Step.
Breathe. Smile.
Step. Step.
Notice the light.
Notice the shadow.
Breathe.
Be here now.

So sweet this walk.
Right here. Right now.
Just breather.
And step.
Left.
Right.
Just breathe.

And sit.
Sounds float.
Thoughts flitter.
Light shines.
Be here now.

Feel the peace.
Feel the love.
Breathe it in.
Pause.

I'm cold. (Is that true?)
Breathe.

So sweet (this practice)
Begin again.
There is no place else to be.

Breathe.
Allow the light to shine on you
And within.

Breathe.
And be grateful for all you have.

Be grateful for the breath.
Be grateful for this community.
Be grateful for the practice.

Be. Here. Now.

Magnificence Unfolding

Divine Order at work.
Releasing old stories
And shedding old patterns
Leaves nothing.
Until the new story
And the new pattern
Take hold.
This process of change is natural and good.
Be not dismayed.
Be not deceived.
Be not distracted.
This is not depression.
It is evolution.
So stay focused on the vision.
Allow the release to complete.
And know you are always
Magnificence Unfolding

Success and Prosperity

i
am a
perfect idea
in Divine Mind.
success
and prosperity
are mine.

I Walk in Peace

Could I just catch a break?
Could I just take a breath?
I know I can handle whatever life presents.
    I am strong.
    I am smart.
    I am resourceful.
    I am resilient.
But right now
I am so tired.
    of worrying
    of hustling
    and just scraping by
I am so tired.
    of settling
    of hiding
    and wanting to cry
I am so tired.
    of shrinking
    of losing
    not understanding why
Could I just catch a break?
Could I just take a breath?
I know I can handle whatever Life presents.
    I Am Peace
    I Am Joy
    I Am Faith
    I Am Love
So right now
I am so alive
    with praying
    with serving
    and daily meditation

I am so alive
    seeing sunrise
    and sunset
    and all of Creation
I am so alive
    being grateful
    and faithful
    without limitation
I am ready to catch my break
I am ready to take this breath.

There is no curve ball to catch.
There is no race to run.
There is no game to lose.
There is no test to fail.

There is only the Law of Attraction
There is only the Law of Cause and Effect
There is only the Law of Love
There is only the Law of Beauty
There is only the Law of Abundance
There is only the Law of Forgiveness
There is only God

So I catch the rhythm of an eternal Life.
I am filled with the warmth of an eternal Breath.
My peace and my prosperity are already present.
I walk in peace.

celebrate your blessings

when special people
come
into your life you must
stop
and acknowledge the gift.
you must
focus
on your growth
through the mirror
they provide.
you must
give
of your love and talents
to enrich their existence.
you must
celebrate
your blessings.

Tweetments

A 'tweetment' is a spiritual mind treatment (affirmative prayer) in the form of a tweet (140 characters or less).

*"We have to pray with our eyes on God,
not on the difficulties."*

Oswald Chambers

Infinite Wisdom.
I am connected.
I have clarity.
Faith not fear.
Grateful & blessed,
I release & let go.
And So It Is.

#smtweetment

There's no limit to the abundance of God.
That abundance is mine.
I have all I need.
Grateful. I let go.
And So It Is.

#smtweetment

There's no limit to the abundance of God.
That abundance is mine.
I have all I need & desire.
Grateful.
I let go.
And So It Is.

#smtweetment

All there is is God.
All I am is God.
My life is God's life.
Grateful for the blessing.
I completely surrender.
And So It Is.

#smtweetment

There is no spot where God is not.
God is here as me.
I live a blessed life.
I'm so grateful! I let it Be.
And So It Is.

#smtweetment

God is perfect health.
I am one with God.
So my true nature is health.
With deep gratitude I let the Law do its work.
Amen.

#smtweetment

Unlimited Love.
I am made of THAT.
All my relationships reflect love.
Gratefully I release this into the Law.
And So It Is.

#smtweetment

God is eternal.
Spirit and I are one.
I don't fear death.
I choose to live life fully!
I gratefully release this to Spirit.

#smtweetment

God's creativity has no limits.
I am an idea in Spirit.
I move through writers' block with ease.
Grateful. Aligned. Surrendered.

#smtweetment

God is Good
& I am God expressing.
Kindness is my way.
So grateful to know & be this Truth.
I let the Law take over completely.

#smtweetment

God is Peace.
I am one w/God.
Worry has no power over me.
Grateful,
I turn this over to the power & presence of the One.

#smtweetment

Resources

"Is prayer your steering wheel or your spare tire?"

Corrie ten Boom

Spiritual Mind Treatment Example

Condition	What old pattern is expressing? What am I experiencing that is not God? What's not working in my life? *Example*: *My spouse has asked for a divorce and my team at work is going through major conflict too.*
Purpose	What new possibility do I want to experience? What spiritual principle would provide healing? What quality of God would be the opposite of the condition? *Example*: *I want to save my marriage if possible and have less stress at work. I want love to prevail. I desire peace & harmony.*

Recognition	I know that God is all there is. God is the perfect example of Harmony and Love. There is no peace greater than the Peace of Spirit.
Unification	There is no separation between me and Spirit. Divine Love is expressed from my essential nature and creates harmony in all my relationships.
Realization	I choose to experience harmony and love in my relationships at home and at work. I am an example of peace in all my conversations. I call forth my essential nature of love as the solution for every thing I see as a problem. Beginning now, I easily express love and I am an example of harmony in action.
Thanksgiving	I am deeply grateful for my understanding of the way the Creative Process works. As I speak this Word I know it is done and I am thankful.
Release	I let go. I let my Higher Power manifest this in my life.
Amen! *or* **And So It Is!** *or* **other closing phrase**	

Helpful Prayer Phrases

As you build your own prayers, here are some phrases that might help you if you are unsure what to say.

Recognition

- God is eternal, changeless and Infinite.
- There is only one Life. That life is God's Life. That Life is perfect. That Life is unlimited and timeless.
- Spirit. Nothing was, is or ever will be created that is not of Spirit.
- I now turn my attention from the form of life to the Inner Divine Formless Spirit that is the core of my being.
- There is only one Mind. It is the clear thinking, all knowing, always loving Mind of God.
- God gives unconditionally. God gives all and gives to all alike.

Unification

- God's Life is my life now.
- This is the same energy that breathes me, moves me and has its being as me.
- I know that I am God in the flesh. God experiences life as, in and through me.
- I have the qualities of God in me at every moment. That is my true, essential nature.
- I am remembering who I am. I am the I Am expressing and experiencing life as me.

Realization

Note: The realization step always reflects the change you want to experience. Describe not only the desired outcome, but how you might feel or what you would be doing differently when your prayer is answered. Just remember, even though you are imagining what it will feel or look like, your description of it in the prayer is always in the present tense.

Thanksgiving

- I am so grateful for the knowledge and understanding of the Spiritual Truth about this situation.

- With deep gratitude I speak my word, knowing it can only be answer with YES!

- I am happy and grateful for the unlimited supply available to me through Spirit.

- I am thankful for the ever expanding expression of God in all aspects of my life.

- It is with joyful gratitude I accept this good unfolding in my life.

Release

- I now let go, knowing the Law is reconfiguring every thing that needs to be changed to bring this Truth into physical form.

- This is already done in the Mind of God and so I release it now.

- I release this into the river of Divine Law knowing it can only flow and grow into its natural demonstration.

- I let it go and let it be.

- I accept this as the Truth and allow it to unfold naturally.

About Faith

For the purpose of this essay, let's define a practitioner as any one who is applying spiritual practices in their life. A practitioner not only has faith, but uses faith in a positive way. The power of faith strengthens each practitioner in his personal life and it also serves as the foundation upon which she can stand when believing the Spiritual Truth for others.

Introduction

In the very first line of "The Practitioner Consciousness" Ernest Holmes said, "The Practitioner has a complete conviction that a higher use of the Law of Cause and Effect transcends a lower use of it."[1] This conviction is an active demonstration of faith.

Faith is often described as belief in evidence unseen. But the faith of a practitioner is made strong by evidence seen again and again and recognized as the omnipresence of God. An effective practitioner not only believes in the presence of Spirit but also uses the power of Spirit to manifest good.

In that way, the practitioner is following the example set by the Master Teacher, Jesus. "He was not merely a man who *had* great faith. He *used* his faith in a positive rather than a negative way. His faith in good was equal to the average man's faith in evil. It was not a different faith; it was a different *use* of faith."[2]

In reality everyone has faith. But there are three questions about faith every practitioner must consider.

1. "What do you have faith in?" Is your faith in the unlimited love of Spirit or in the limitations of humanity?

---

[1] Holmes, Ernest. "The Practitioner Consciousness"
[2] Holmes, Ernest. "How to Use the Science of Mind (Function of Faith, page 43) Published 1950. © Science of Mind Publishing, 2005.

2. "How does your faith show up in not only what you think but also in what you do and say?"

3. "Are you committed to sharing your faith with others – even (or maybe especially) those who have no faith but yours to rely on?"

The seed of faith is planted first within the life and experience of each practitioner. Nurturing the seed with daily practice is like feeding the seed of a plant with the basics of sunshine, soil and water that it needs to grow. Fertilizing the growing plant of faith with prayer and with deeper study during times of doubt or stress might be compared with periodic replanting of a growing fern. As the plant grows, its roots expand and need to be moved into a larger container. As a practitioner's faith grows, his container (or life) also expands. And even after faith has grown strong and is a tangible part of the Practitioner's life, it still requires attention, for as it ages and deepens it reveals nuances unimagined in the early stages. Just like a seed becomes a strong, sturdy oak tree able to withstand wind, storms and seasons of change; a practitioner who has nurtured the growth of faith will rely on it to get through challenges and fears through all seasons of life.

"Faith speaks when hope dissembles. Faith lives when hope dies dead." (Algernon Charles Swinburne) A practitioner knows that faith is more than hope. Hope allows for disappointment. Hope implies there is a possibility that whatever is desired may not happen. But faith transforms hope into certainty and allows no room for questioning that good must come from whatever is being experienced.

When a practitioner lives in faith it becomes a natural expression to recognize the God presence in every one and every thing. When a practitioner faces adversity guided by faith, she realizes the current life challenge is part of a bigger journey.

It is not a punishment for some past behavior as much as it is preparation for a future opportunity.

"Seasons are not stages … They are neither linear nor chartable. They do not begin and end at predictable times, and no two seasons are alike. Seasons are cyclical. We move in and out of them a thousand times as our spirits grow and stretch."[3]

It is our faith that becomes the constant no matter what season we are experiencing. Living live in this way, the practitioner learns, through his own example, that faith is the safest boat to ride during both calm waters and tempestuous seas. Faith becomes the safe harbor no matter what is occurring in one's life.

Joel Goldsmith reminds us, "God is just as much on the other side of this door as He is on this side. There is no place where I can go today where the presence of God is not. Wherever I am, God is."[4] Being a practitioner is simply living and serving from this belief and having faith that because this is true there is no separation between God and self or between God and anyone you might be speaking a prayer for.

As a practitioner it is as important to show the way as it is to tell the way. Practitioners do teach about spiritual Truth and faith; it is a valuable skill to be able to educate others about what faith is. But it is more important to demonstrate ways to apply faith in daily life because our family members, friends and colleagues learn from observation as well.

A practitioner has "an unqualified faith that the law works for us as we work with It."[5] What does it mean to have an unqualified faith? It means we are definite, absolutely sure, unmovable and

---

[3] Weems, Renita. "Listening for God: A Minister's Journey through Silence and Doubt" Simon and Schuster, 1999
[4] Goldsmith, Joel. "Practicing the Presence: The Inspirational Guide to Regaining Meaning and a Sense of Purpose in Your Life" ©1958, 1986. HarperCollins, 1991
[5] Holmes, Ernest. "Science of Mind" (47-1)

totally convinced that God is for us, not against us. It means we believe, and behave as if, "life is neither separate from God nor different from Good. Life is God, and Good is the only power this is, or can be."[6]

When someone asks you to pray for them, they are depending on your faith to be so strong it can cause change. A skilled practitioner is able to identify known or unknown beliefs that are generating undesired results and then, through active faith, set a new cause into action. This is no small task but it is made easier when faith is strong because the practitioner knows it is Universal Law that is doing the work, making the change and creating a new future.

Summary

In the book, "The Faith Club" three women, Ranya, Suzanne and Priscilla share their journey learning from each other about the similarities and the differences between their different religions. In a discussion about faith I came to the following conclusion:

> *Priscilla*: I think faith is sometimes just the act of getting up in the morning, putting both feet on the floor and standing up.

> *Ranya*: Yes. And faith is not the domain of one group or another. It belongs to anyone who chooses to have it. It doesn't have to have a label or a name.

> *Suzanne*: And it doesn't have to be sanctioned by any authority.

> *Ranya*: Ultimately it's a choice we make as individuals – to have faith.[7]

---

[6] Holmes, Ernest. "Science of Mind" (487-7) ©1938 Holmes. Tarcher/Putnum, 1998
[7] Idliby, Ranya, Suzanne Oliver & Priscilla Warner. "The Faith Club" Simon & Schuster, 2006

And so, it is the practitioner's choice to have faith in Good. And it becomes the practitioner's responsibility to demonstrate that faith daily, not only to have a better life herself; but also to help others experience a life worth living.

"Give faith to one another, for faith and hope and mercy are yours to give."[8]

---

[8] "A Course in Miracles (1975) Foundation for Inner Peace

Quotations about Prayer

"Prayer is not an old woman's idle amusement. Properly understood and applied, it is the most potent instrument of action."
— Mahatma Gandhi

"Don't pray when it rains if you don't pray when the sun shines."
— Leroy "Satchel" Paige

"Prayer is not asking. Prayer is putting oneself in the hands of God, at His disposition, and listening to His voice in the depth of our hearts."
— Mother Teresa

"You pray in your distress and in your need; would that you might pray also in the fullness of your joy and in your days of abundance."
— Kahlil Gibran

"Why must people kneel down to pray? If I really wanted to pray I'll tell you what I'd do. I'd go out into a great big field all alone or in the deep, deep woods and I'd look up into the sky—up—up—up—into that lovely blue sky that looks as if there was no end to its blueness. And then I'd just feel a prayer."
— L.M. Montgomery

"We tend to use prayer as a last resort, but God wants it to be our first line of defense. We pray when there's nothing else we can do, but God wants us to pray before we do anything at all."
— Oswald Chambers

"Is prayer your steering wheel or your spare tire?"
— Corrie ten Boom

"I have so much to do that I shall spend the first three hours in prayer."
— Martin Luther

"Do not have your concert first, and then tune your instrument afterwards. Begin the day with the Word of God and prayer, and get first of all into harmony with Him."
— James Hudson Taylor

"The reality of loving God is loving him like he's a Superhero who actually saved you from stuff rather than a Santa Claus who merely gave you some stuff."
— Criss Jami

"The only difference between a wish and a prayer is that you're at the mercy of the universe for the first, and you've got some help with the second."
— Jodi Picoult

"It doesn't matter how you pray--with your head bowed in silence, or crying out in grief, or dancing. Churches are good for prayer, but so are garages and cars and mountains and showers and dance floors."
— Anne Lamott

"The wise man in the storm prays God not for safety from danger but for deliverance from fear."
— Ralph Waldo Emerson

"I think the reason we sometimes have the false sense that God is so far away is because that is where we have put him. We have kept him at a distance, and then when we are in need and call on him in prayer, we wonder where he is. He is exactly where we left him."
— Ravi Zacharias

"We have to pray with our eyes on God, not on the difficulties."
— Oswald Chambers

"When I pray for another person, I am praying for God to open my eyes so that I can see that person as God does, and then enter into the stream of love that God already directs toward that person."
— Philip Yancey

"I have been driven many times upon my knees by the overwhelming conviction that I had no where else to go. My own wisdom and that of all about me seemed insufficient for that day."
— Abraham Lincoln

The sovereign cure for worry is prayer.
— William James

Prayer is simply a two-way conversation between you and God.
— Billy Graham

"The goal of prayer is to live all of my life and speak all of my words in the joyful awareness of the presence of God.
Prayer becomes real when we grasp the reality and goodness of God's constant presence with 'the real me.' Jesus lived his everyday life in conscious awareness of his Father."
— John Ortberg Jr.

"The function of prayer is not to influence God, but rather to change the nature of the one who prays."
— Søren Kierkegaard

Tracy Brown

"You always have a choice."

That's been my personal motto for more than 40 years. And while all my choices didn't turn out so well I always knew if I wanted to have a different outcome then it was up to me to make a different choice.

Just like you, I've had high highs and low lows. I've leaned on others and have had others lean on me. There have been times I've had money and times when I didn't. I've fallen down and I've gotten up.

I've enjoyed great success in corporate settings. I've been immersed in operations of nonprofit organizations through years of volunteer work and board service. I've owned and operated a training and consulting firm, lived in several states and traveled a lot. And I'm the author of several books who roller skates as often as possible.

It is this variety of life experience - combined with the rigorous training - that prepares me to meet you wherever you are and help you define, then live, the life you dream of.

For More Information:

- www.TracyBrownRScP.com
- www.ReclaimJoy.com
- www.StainedGlassSpirit.net

Also by Tracy Brown

Reclaim Joy! A Journal to Help You Record, Recall and Remember to Celebrate the Joy in Your Life

Reveal Joy! A Journal to Help You Notice and Nurture Your Natural State of Joy

Leadership

Leaderthink: Inspiring Reminders to Think, and Act, Like a Leader (Volume 1)

Leaderthink: Inspiring Reminders to Think, and Act, Like a Leader (Volume 2)

Diversity & Inclusion

71 Ways to Demonstrate Commitment to Diversity

71 Ways to Inspire Commitment to Diversity and Inclusion

71 Ways to Create a Culture for Diversity and Inclusion

Diagnosis Diversity: Maximizing Diversity in Health Care

motiVersity: Motivating While Valuing Diversity

Breaking the Barrier of Bias: The Subtle Influence of Bias and What to Do About It

> Joy. Beauty. Abundance. Balance. Peace. Wisdom. Love.
> Wellness. Prosperity. Safety. Creativity. Harmony. Wholeness.
>
> *You deserve it all.*
> Let me help you live the life you dream of!

Coaching Services

Spiritual Shift Coaching Package
This package includes four one-hour sessions of one-on-one coaching.

Change Your Thinking – Change Your Life Package
Get clarity and watch miracles happen in your life. Choose this 9-session package that starts with a 2-hour strategy session and includes a bonus of 3 visioning sessions to help you tap into deeper guidance for the next phase of your life.

CBAR: Conceive, Believe, Achieve, Receive Package
Invest in yourself and create the life you've always wanted. This 18 session package includes 12 one-hour and six 30-minute coaching sessions plus a 2-hour strategy session and a bonus of 3 visioning sessions.

VIP Intensive
This is a one-day transformation and strategy session custom designed for your needs.

For more information, visit:

www.TracyBrownRScP.com
or

www.YourNextBestYou.com

Made in the USA
San Bernardino, CA
04 November 2017